Strong Meat
for Christians

Strong Meat
for Christians

Compiled by A.N. Bazalgette

Edited by Karen Friday Randall

Illustrated by Morgan Davidson

Peppermill Press © 2016

STRONG MEAT
FOR CHRISTIANS

Copyright © Bazalgette 2016

All Rights Reserved

ISBN: 978-0-692-80479-7

First Published 2016 by
Peppermill Press

Illustrated by Morgan Davidson
www.morgandavidsonart.com

Printed and bound in Florida, USA by
Whitehall Printing Company
www.whitehallprinting.com

TABLE OF CONTENTS

PREFACE

For when for the time ye ought to be teachers, ye have need that one teach you again which be the first principles of the oracles of God; and are become such as have need of milk, and not of strong meat. For everyone that useth milk is unskilled in the word of righteousness: for he is a babe. But strong meat belongeth to them that are of full age, even those who by reason of use have their senses exercised to discern both good and evil.

Hebrews 5:12-14 KJV

What food is strong meat? I think two words of our Lord – one to Satan – the other to His disciples, give the perfect answer. *"Man shall live by every word that proceedeth out of the mouth of God."* (Matthew 4:4) Every word – not only the comfortable words....is it not possible that some among us are babes still, satisfied with "milk" (that is to say, the part of the revelation of God which appears to make little demand upon us). And that we have never whole heartedly gone on to take the food that is meant for us, the strong meat that our Lord and His warriors all down the ages lived upon; and for that reason we have failed to grow up?

Amy Carmichael (1867-1951)
Thou Givest – They Gather

Milk is something that is first digested by the mother. It refers to indirect revelations, revelations that do not come to a person directly. A man who drinks milk cannot receive any direct revelation from God. He receives revelation from other spiritual men, who transfer such revelation to him.

Watchman Nee (1903-1972)
How to Study the Bible

Soldiers

It matters a good deal that your book-food should be strong meat. We are what we think about. Think about trivial things or weak things and somehow one loses fibre and becomes flabby in spirit. Soldiers need to be strong.

Amy Carmichael (1867-1951)
Candles in the Dark

Epigram

On parent knees, a naked new born child, weeping thou sat'st while all around thee smiled; so live, that sinking to thy life's last sleep, calm thou may'st smile, whilst all around thee weep.

Sir William Jones (1746-1794)

Chapter 1

God's Ultimate Purpose

...when the times have reached their fulfilment to bring all things in heaven and on earth together under one head even Jesus Christ.

Ephesians 1:10
New International Version

I pray also for those who will believe in Me through their message, that all of them may be one, Father, just as You are in Me and I am in You. May they also be in us, so that the world may believe that You have sent me. I have given them the glory that You gave Me, that they may be one as we are one. I in them and You in Me...

Father, I want those you have given Me to be with Me where I am and to see My glory, the glory You have given Me because You loved Me before the creation of the world.

John 17:20-24 NIV

The perfect harmony that will be restored will be harmony in man, and between men – Harmony in heaven and all under the blessed Lord Jesus Christ, Who will be the Head of all! Everything will again be united *in* Him. And wonder of wonders, marvelous beyond compare – when all this happens, it will never be undone again. All will be reunited *in* Him to all eternity. That is the message. That is God's plan. That is the mystery which has been revealed unto us...Do you know that these things are so marvelous that you will never hear anything greater either in this world or in the world to come?

D. Martin Lloyd Jones (1900-1981)
God's Ultimate Purpose

All this is from God, who reconciled us to Himself through Christ and gave us the ministry of reconciliation: that God was reconciling the world to Himself in Christ – not counting men's sins against them.

2 Corinthians 5:18-19 NIV

...and gave us the ministry whose work is that of proclaiming the message of this reconciliation, namely, that absolute deity in Christ was reconciling the world [of sinners] to Himself...

2 Corinthians 5:18-19 Expanded Version

...for until I become one substance with Him, I can never have love, rest, or true bliss; that is to say that until I am so bound to Him that there may be no created thing between my God and me ...And who shall do this deed? Truly, Himself, by His mercy and His grace, for He made me and blessedly restored me to that end.

Julian of Norwich (1342-1416)
Revelations of Divine Love

...and where He says, "I shall," I take it for the unity of the Holy Trinity, three persons in one truth; and where He says, 'You shall see for yourself.' I understand it as the referring to the union with the Holy Trinity of all mankind who shall be saved. And with these sayings God wishes to be surrounded by rest and peace; and thus Christ's spiritual thirst comes to an end; for this is the spiritual thirst, the love-longing that lasts and ever shall do until we see that revelation on Judgment Day.

For we that shall be saved, and shall be Christ's joy and His bliss, are still here on earth, and shall be until that last day. Therefore this is the thirst, the incompleteness of His bliss, that He does not have us *in* Himself as wholly as He will have then...Thus He has pity and compassion for us, and He has longing to have us, but His wisdom and love do not permit the end to come until the best time.

Julian of Norwich (1342-1416)
Revelations of Divine Love

Then the end will come, when He hands over the Kingdom of God the Father after He has destroyed all dominion, authority and power. For He must reign until He has put all His enemies under His feet...When He has done this, then the Son Himself will be made subject to Him who put everything under him, so that God may be all in all.

1 Corinthians 15:24-25, 28 NIV

Chapter 2

God's Love for Me

Love is that liquor sweet and most divine,
Which my God feels as blood, but I as wine.

George Herbert

God so loved, so unsparingly, as to do to His Son's body and soul the injury of the Cross. That is the principle on which God's love dealt with the vast evil of the world. He reserved for Himself what He forbade Abraham to do.

Oswald Chambers (1874-1917)
Conformed to His Image

Why was Jesus Christ made flesh?

Love was the intrinsic motive. Christ is God-man because He was a lover of man. Christ came out of pity and indulgence to us. Not our deserts, but our misery made Christ take flesh. Christ's taking flesh was a plot of free grace, and a pure design of love. Christ incarnate is nothing but love covered with flesh.

Thomas Watson (1620-1686)
A Body of Divinity

When, therefore, the first spark of a desire after God arises in thy soul, *cherish it with all thy care,* give all thy heart unto it; it is nothing less than a touch of the divine Loadstone that is to draw thee out of the vanity of time, into the riches of eternity. It will do for thee, as the star did for them; it will lead thee to the birth of Jesus, not in a stable at Bethlehem in Judea, but to the birth of Jesus in the dark center of thine own fallen soul.

William Law (1686-1761)
The Spirit of Prayer

I pray that out of His glorious riches He may strengthen you with power through His Spirit in your inner being, so that Christ may dwell in your hearts through faith. And I pray that you, being rooted and established in love, may have power, together with all the saints, to grasp how wide and long and high and deep is the love of Christ, and to know this love that surpasses knowledge – that you may be filled to the measure of all the fullness of God.

Ephesians 3:16-19 NIV

We find ourselves, as it were, upon the <u>pinnacle of Christian truth</u>. There is nothing higher than this.

D. Martyn Lloyd-Jones (1900-1981)
The Unsearchable Riches of Christ

God has an *attractive virtue* which draws the soul more and more powerfully to Himself, and in attracting, He purifies.

Madame Guyon (1648-1717)
Experiencing the Depths of Jesus Christ

It is impossible my beloved hearers, to express the profound and the ardent affection, and the intense desire there is in Christ, to regain possession of our hearts, to have us again near Him, and to bind and unite us eternally to Himself and Himself to us. Angels and men cannot comprehend it, but will adore this mystery with the profoundest admiration, to all eternity. The spirit of Christ, which dwells in believers, desires us, even to jealousy: He cannot bear that a heart that cost Him so dear, that a heart, which He loves to such a degree should still cleave to other objects, and not remain wholly and solely devoted to Him. He loves the soul as though He loved naught besides; and she must love Him in the same manner, in return; ...The love of Christ touches the soul, and attracts her to itself and she follows this attraction.

Gerhard Tersteegen (1697-1769)
Letters and Writings

This theme of the love of Christ is something of which the man who is not a Christian, has no conception at all.....There is a secret element in this matter. It is a secret that is only enjoyed by the Lord's people...the hidden manna! The white stone with a name written on it that nobody can understand except the recipient! Others see the lettering but it means nothing to them. None understand it but those who really receive it. This is that *secret love* no one else knows.

Martin Lloyd-Jones (1900-1981)
The Unsearchable Riches of Christ

The Lord hath appeared of old unto me, saying, Yea, I have loved thee with an everlasting love: therefore with loving-kindness have I drawn thee.

Jeremiah 31:3 KJV

On the other hand, the Deity, as considered in itself and without the soul of man, has an infinite, unchangeable tendency of love and desire toward the soul of man, to unite, and communicate its own riches and glory to it.

William Law (1686-1761)
The Spirit of Prayer

...And in this vision he showed me a little thing – the size of a hazel nut, lying in the palm of my hand, and to my mind's eye, it was as round as any ball. I looked at it and thought, "What can this be?" And the answer came to me – "It is all that is made." I wondered how it could last for it was so small that I thought it might suddenly disappear. And the answer in my mind was, It lasts and will last forever, because God loves it – and in the same way, everything exists through the love of God."

Julian of Norwich (1342-1416)
Revelations of Divine Love

Who would not desire to take His lot with the servants of a Master whose boundless love fills all holy minds with astonishment?

C.H. Spurgeon (1834-1892)
The Treasury of David
Commentary on Psalm 31:19

The things that make God dear to us are not so much His great big blessings as the tiny things, because they show His amazing intimacy with us; He knows every detail of our individual lives.

Oswald Chambers (1874-1917)
My Utmost for His Highest

This love or desire of God toward the soul of man is so great that He <u>gave</u> His only begotten Son – The Gospel is the history of the love of God to man.

William Law (1686-1761)
The Spirit of Prayer

I will betroth you to me forever;
I will betroth you in righteousness and justice,
        in love and compassion.
I will betroth you in faithfulness,
        and you will acknowledge the Lord.

Hosea 2:19-20 NIV

A superlative verse. A bottomless mine of love, It is more suitable to be enjoyed in silence than to be expounded in words.

C.H. Spurgeon (1834-1892)
Spurgeon's Devotional Bible
Hosea 2:19-20

A Carol

...For in His lovely baby days
        Heaven's door was set ajar.
And angels flew through glimmering ways
        And lit a silver star.
No need for halo or for crown
        To show the King of Love come down
To dwell where sinners are.

But when He died upon the Rood,
        The King of Glory, He
There was no star, there was no good
        Nor any majesty.
For diadem was only scorn,
        A twisted torturing crown of thorns
And it was all for me.

Amy Carmichael (1867-1951)
Toward Jerusalem

Then he turned toward the woman and said to Simon, "Do you see this woman? I came into your house. You did not give me any water for my feet, but she wet my feet with her tears and wiped them with her hair. You did not give me a kiss but this woman from the time I entered has not stopped kissing my feet. You did not put oil on my head, but she has poured perfume on my feet. Therefore, I tell you, her many sins have been forgiven - for she loved much."

Luke 7:44-47 NIV

Thou Gavest Me No Kiss

And may we all be Thine own Maries, Lord?
Dear worthy Lord, how courteous Love's reward;
For all the little that I give to Thee,
Thou gavest first to me.

Rich is thy harvest, O Thou Corn of Wheat,
A cloud of lovers gather round Thy feet;
What miracle of love that Thou should'st miss
Low on Thy feet, one kiss.

Amy Carmichael (1867-1951)
Toward Jerusalem

The Inheritance

Am I not enough, Mine own? Enough
Mine own, for thee?
Hath the world its palace towers,
Garden glades of magic flowers,
Where thou fain woulds't be?
Fair things and false are there,
False things but fair.
All shalt thou find at last,
Only in Me.
Am I not enough? Mine own? I, for ever,
and alone, I, *needing thee*?

Gerhard Tersteegen (1697-1769)
Hymns of Tersteegen and Others

How often have you and I shamefully spurned and rejected his proffered kindness and love; and yet He was not weary of seeking us? O how tenderly does He love, even before He is beloved! but still how infinitely more tenderly, when He has attained His object, and when He can forever betroth himself with the soul, as with a bride, and affiance Himself to her in righteousness! This is often succeeded by many precious and even *sensible* communications of His love to the soul. Christ presents her with many invaluable jewels and celestial blessings, and gives her to experience, in her measure, "righteousness" peace and joy in the Holy Ghost."

Gerhard Tersteegen (1697-1769)
Letters and Writings

Christ loves us also, and loves us voluntarily, with the most tender, ardent, and transporting love of a bridegroom. O yes, the love of Christ really <u>sues</u> for the hearts of poor, lost sinners; and how long must He frequently woo us, before he receives from us the desired consent!

Gerhard Tersteegen (1697-1769)
Letters and Writings

Remember, O lord, Your tender mercies and Your loving-kindnesses; for they are from old.

Psalm 25:6 NKJ

They are the virgin honey of language; for sweetness no words can excel them; but as for the gracious favors which are intended by them, language fails to describe them.

C.H. Spurgeon (1834-1892)
The Treasury of David
Commentary on Psalm 25:6

His *most loved* are often His most tried. The lentil stones and pillars of His New Jerusalem suffer more knocks of God's hammer and tool than the common side-wall stones.

Samuel Rutherford (1600-1661)
Letter CXII
To Mr. John Fergushill

He (God) is the source of all good, and alone sufficient to satisfy us, both in time and eternity. But this being the case, He likewise desires from us, that we should resign all other delights, and venture that which is most dear and precious to us, from cordial love to Him, who is such a faithful friend, and who is invariably so near to us; who, from grace alone, has forgiven us our sins, and called us with a holy calling, in order that He alone may be our treasure. All for all, that is the whole matter; yet still it is not a purchase, but a voluntary love offering on both sides.

Gerhard Tersteegen (1697-1769)
Letters and Writings
Select Letters (Letter IV)

The Temple

...but as pomanders* and wood
    still are good,
Yet being bruised are better scented;
    God to show how far *His love*
could improve,
    Here, as broken, is presented.

George Herbert (1593-1638)
The Banquet (Communion)

* pomanders – oranges or apples, studded with cloves and hung in a closet to perfume the air

Fulfill Me Now

Father of spirits, this my sovereign plea
I bring again and yet again to Thee,

Fulfil me now with love, that I may know
A daily inflow, a daily overflow.

For love, for love my Lord was crucified
With cords of love He bound me to His side.

Pour through me now; I yield myself to Thee,
Love, blessed Love, do as thou wilt with me.

Amy Carmichael (1867-1951)
Toward Jerusalem

I see also, that to live a life of grace, it is needful that we feel daily – that *love-on the side of God* – is the *only* reason why gracious feelings are ever experienced by us. Why is the fire kindled after going out every morning in my room? Just because I like to have its heat. So the Lord daily kindles love to Himself *in* me – just because He never ceases to desire that I should be His.

Andrew Bonar (1810-1892)
Diary and Life

But Noah found favor in the eyes of the Lord.

Genesis 6:8 NIV

God's description of a saint, then, is one that has found favor in His sight. And this is the saint's own account of himself - ...'then was I in His eyes as one that found favor.' (Song of Solomon 8:10 KJV) This is all he can say for himself – all the account he can give of the origin of his sonship, the cause of his spiritual change. How blessed to be able thus simply to trace all that is good in us directly to the sovereign will and love of Jehovah!

Horatius Bonar (1808-1889)
Thoughts on Genesis

I consider myself as the most wretched of men, full of sores and corruption, and who has committed all sorts of crimes against his King; touched with a sensible regret, I confess to Him all my wickedness, I ask His forgiveness, I abandon myself in His hands that He may do what He pleases with me. The King, full of mercy and goodness, very far from chastising me, embraces me with love, makes me eat at His table, serves me with His own hands, gives me the key of His treasures. He converses and delights Himself with me incessantly, in a thousand and a thousand ways, and treats me in all respects as His favorite. It is thus I consider myself from time to time in His holy presence.

Brother Lawrence (1614-1691)

Love

Love bade me welcome. Yet my soul drew back.
    Guilty of dust and sin.
But quick-eyed Love, observing me grow slack
    From my first entrance in
Drew nearer to me, sweetly questioning,
    If I lacked anything.

A guest, I answered, worthy to be here:
    Love said, You shall be he.
I the unkind, ungrateful? Ah, my dear,
    I cannot look on thee.
Love took my hand, and smiling did reply.
    Who made the eyes but I?
Truth, Lord, but I have marred them: let my shame
    Go where it doth deserve.
And know you not, says Love, who bore the blame?
    My dear, then I will serve.
You must sit down, says, Love, and taste my meat:
    So I did sit and eat.

George Herbert (1593-1633)

My God, what is a heart,
That Thou shoulds't it so eye and woo
Pouring upon it all Thy art,
As if Thou hadst nothing else to do?

George Herbert (1593-1633)
From Matins
The Poems of George Herbert

I speak not this as if I thought ye had forgotten what God did, to have your love long since, but that ye may awake yourself in this sleepy age and remember fruitfully Christ's first suiting of your love, both with fire and water, and try if He got his answer, or if ye be yet to give it to Him.

Samuel Rutherford (1600-1661)
Letter LXXII
To William Gordon of Roberton

Chapter 3

Christianity

It is the effectual working of the power of God that makes anyone a Christian. It means a rebirth, a regeneration. It is not the result of our decision; it is not something that you and I decide to do. It is what happens to us! "The effectual workings of His power!"

D. Martin Lloyd-Jones
Ephesians 3

This is the Christianity that began with the Fall, and has been preached ever since to every son of fallen Man - in every Corner of the World - and by the same Preacher - that tells every Man:

that he ought to be better than he is.

For was not Man fallen from a better State than that he is now in - he could no more be ashamed or offended at anything that his Nature prompts him to do, than the Ox is ashamed at breaking into a good Pasture.

Every Man, therefore - from the beginning of the world - has had Christianity and the Gospel written and preached within him - as it contains the Fall of Man, and his need of being raised to a better State.

William Law (1686-1761)
The Way to Divine Knowledge
First Dialogue

Now the right ground of understanding the true meaning of every different expression – relating to Christ, as our Savior, or salvation, lies in these two things:

1. what Christ is i*n Himself*
2. what He does or intends to do f*or us*.

Everything that is said of His birth, His life, His sufferings, His death, His resurrection and ascension – are all of them both with respect of God and ourselves – of one and the same effectiveness – full of one and the same end:

1. to destroy in man the works of the devil
2. and to make all that died in Adam alive again *in* Christ.

William Law (1686-1761)
Letters

For nothing could possibly be the redemption or recovery of man but *regeneration* alone. Man's misery was his having lost the life and light of heaven from his soul, and therefore nothing in all the universe of nature, but a *new birth* of that which he had lost, could be his deliverance from a fallen state.

William Law (1686-1761)
The Spirit of Prayer

In reply, Jesus declared "I tell you the truth, no one can see the Kingdom of God unless he is born again!"

John 3:3 NIV

Therefore, if anyone is in Christ, he is a new creation; the old has gone, the new has come!

2 Corinthians 5:17 NIV

God cannot part with His grace, or goodness, or strength, as an external thing that He gives us – as He gives the raindrops from heaven. No; He can only give it, and we can only enjoy it, as He works it Himself directly and unceasingly. And the only reason that He does not work it more effectually and continuously is – that we do not let Him.

Andrew Murray (1828-1917)
Waiting on God

A Christ not *in* us is the same thing as a Christ not *ours*. If we are only so *far* with Christ, as to own and receive the history of His birth, person, and character – if *this* is all we have of Him – we are as much without Him, as much left to ourselves, as little helped by Him, as those evil spirits which cried out. "We know who Thou art, the Holy One of God." – for those evil spirits and all the fallen angels, are totally without Christ, and have no benefit from Him – for this one and only reason – because Christ is not *in* them – nothing of the Son of God is generated or born *in them.*

William Law (1686-1761)
Wholly for God

Highly Favored in the Beloved

The Apostle uses the same word in respect to us, as the archangel used about the Virgin Mary, 'Hail, thou that art highly favored.' That meant that God had chosen Mary of all the women in the world to bear his Son. She had been created for this, that the Son of God should enter her womb and be born of her. The Apostle speaks similarly of us. He has already told us that we have been predestined unto the adoption of Sons. But it is greater even then than that. Not only are we made sons of God, but Christ comes *into* us – Christ *in* you, the hope of glory (Colossians 1:27) As He had physically entered into Mary, so spiritually he enters into every one of us who are his children.

Dr. Martin Lloyd-Jones (1900-1981)
God Ultimate Purpose

Never make a principle out of your experience; let God be as original with other people as He is with you.

Oswald Chambers (1874-1917)
My Utmost for His Highest

Hence also it is, that in the Christian Church, there have been in all ages – amongst the most illiterate – both men and women – who have attained to a deep understanding of the mysteries of the wisdom and love of God in Christ Jesus. And what wonder? Since it is not Art or Science, or skill in grammar or logic – but the opening of the Divine Life *in* the soul – that can give true understanding of the things of God.

William Law (1686-1761)
The Spirit of Prayer

But when He, the Spirit of truth comes. He will guide you into all truth.

John 16:13 NIV

There is no lukewarmness in hell. There is no lukewarmness in heaven. Lukewarmness is found in the church.

Andrew Bonar (1810-1892)
Heavenly Springs

In what are you to find your salvation?

Not in any historic faith, or knowledge of anything absent or distant from you: not in any formality of opinion about faith and works, repentance, forgiveness of sins, or justification and sanctification; not in any truth or righteousness that you can have from yourself, from the best of men or books; but wholly and solely in the life of God, or Christ of God, quickened and born again *in* you.

William Law (1686-1761)
The Spirit of Love

New birth refers not only to a man's eternal salvation, it means infinitely more than being delivered from sin and from hell. The gift of the essential nature of God is made efficacious in us by the entering in of the Holy Spirit; He imparts to us the quickening life of the Son of God, and we are lifted into the domain where Jesus lives.

Oswald Chambers (1874-1917)
A New Testament Walk

Tolerance is the virtue of those who don't believe in anything.

Unknown

The godly, like candles, light each other.

Paul Byne
The Treasury of David

Sadducees may deny the resurrection – but after Christ raised Lazarus out of the grave, Lazarus can hardly deny it. He had experience of Christ's power in raising the dead – natural men know neither the Spirit or His work.

Samuel Rutherford (1600-1661)
The Power of Faith and Prayer

The Pharisee is much more common than you think. Many Christians try to lead "good, Christian lives" and are proud of themselves for it. They may pray, tithe, and lead moral lives, but inside they are attached to their own ability to live the Christian life. You have hidden (or not so hidden) pride at your own strength. You take pleasure in seeing yourself as strong and good and righteous.

François Fénelon (1651-1714)
The Seeking Heart

The holy cheerfulness of Christians is their beauty and a great ornament to their profession.

Matthew Henry (1662-1715)
Isaiah 61

There are far more people made to think by seeing a believer's joy than by any words he may speak.

Andrew Bonar (1810-1892)

That Christ may dwell in your hearts through faith.

Ephesians 3:17 NIV

'By faith.' What does that mean exactly? Once more we come across a type of teaching which has caused many to stumble and has kept them from the living experience we are considering. 'By faith' does not mean (I use the current phrase) 'take it by faith,' to which we have already referred to briefly. This teaches, concerning this or any other experience in the Christian life, that it is 'quite simple,' you 'just take it by faith'; you just 'open the door to Christ,' and He is in your heart immediately. Though you may feel nothing at all, you must convince yourself that because the Word says that if you open the door He will enter in, therefore, if you opened the door, He must have entered! That you feel nothing is quite immaterial; they say you must go on reckoning and assuming that He has entered because He says He will do so. Such teaching is completely wrong. No teaching is so calculated to rob us of the most exalted experiences in the Christian life; and for this reason – that it is nothing but a form of self-persuasion, the putting into practice of the psychological principle of auto-suggestion. What makes it particularly wrong in this connection is that we are not dealing here with an influence, but with a Person.

Martin Lloyd-Jones (1900-1981)
The Unsearchable Riches of Christ

The best part of Christian work is that part which only God sees.

Andrew Bonar (1810-1892)
Heavenly Springs

Do not try to put religion in the place of Christ. The heart of religion is to know Christ and to know Him better, and to know Him still better. Then to see Him as He is, and then to be made like Him.

Andrew Bonar (1810-1892)
Heavenly Springs

The devil does not care how many hospitals we build, anymore than he cares how many schools and colleges we put up, if only he can pull our ideals down, and side track us onto anything of any sort except the living of holy, humble lives, and the bringing of men, women, and children to know our Lord Jesus Christ not only as Saviour but as Sovereign Lord.

Amy Carmichael (1867-1951)
A Chance to Die

If we are Christians, we are lovers of God, we delight in Him...we delight in the law of God. We do not obey it as a task.... His commandments are not grievous. That constitutes one of the best tests of whether we are Christian or not. Do we have to force ourselves to live the Christian life? Do we enjoy Christian living? Do we wish to be more Christ-like, day by day? These are the tests and they are test of love...the whole object of the law is love first, your relationship to God, then your relationship to your fellow man. It is all a matter of love....the essence of holiness is love.

Dr. Martin Lloyd- Jones (1900-1991)
God's Ultimate Purpose

The Church is a separated body of people who are united to God by the regenerating power of the Spirit, and the bedrock of membership in the Church is that we know who Jesus is by *personal revelation of Him*. The indwelling Spirit is the supreme Guide, and He keeps us absorbed with our Lord. The emphasis today is placed on the furtherance of an organization; the motto is "we must keep this thing going." If we are in God's order the thing will go; if we are not in His order, it won't.

Oswald Chambers (1874-1917)
Conformed to His image

If grace is God's answer – (the gift of Jesus and His life) – then we cannot for a moment dispense with following Christ. But if grace is the data (known facts from which conclusions can be drawn) for my Christian life, it means that I set out to live the Christian life in the world with all my sins justified beforehand. I can go out and sin as much as I like, and rely on His grace to forgive me, for after all, the world is justified in principle by grace. I can therefore cling to my bourgeois secular existence, and remain as I was before, but with the added assurance that the grace of God will cover me. It is under the influence of this kind of "grace" that the world has been made "Christian" but at the cost of secularizing the Christian religion.

When he spoke of grace, Luther always implied as an additional conclusion, that it cost him his own life – which was now for the first time – subjected to the absolute obedience to Christ. Only so could he speak of grace.....judged by the standard of Luther's doctrine, that of his followers was unassailable, and yet – their belief spelt the end and destruction of the Reformation as the revelation on earth of the costly grace of God. The justification of the sinner in the world degenerated into the justification of sin and the world. Costly grace was turned into cheap grace, without discipleship. (following Christ)

Dietrich Bonhoeffer (1906-1945)
The Cost of Discipleship

I know my sheep and my sheep know me – just as the Father knows me and I know the Father – and I lay down my life for the sheep.

John 10:14-15 NIV

...by what painful discipline was He instructed in this knowledge, subjected himself to the wants of every sheep, every lamb of His fold that he might be able to be touched with a feeling of their infirmities?

Theodosia A. Howard (1800-1836)
Viscountess Powerscourt
Letters and Papers

The Lord is my shepherd. I shall not want.

Psalm 23:1 KJV

There is a peace of fullness of expression in this little sentence known only to the sheep....our shepherd has learned the wants of his sheep by experience, for He was himself "led like a lamb to the slaughter".

Theodosia A. Howard (1800-1836)
Viscountess Powerscourt
Letters and Papers

Six Marks of Christ's Sheep

1.   They know their shepherd;
2.   They know His voice;
3.   They hear Him calling each by name;
4.   They love him;
5.   They trust Him;
6.   They follow Him.

Mrs. Rogers

Yea, but words fit to turn the heart, a language to the soul that the sheep of Christ, and they only, could know and follow, was only in Christ's mouth. It is all gibberish and barbarian language that prophets or apostles speak to the heart, until Christ gives out the word – the heart of the Beloved knows the voice of her Husband among a thousand - "the voice of my beloved" (Song 2:8)

Samuel Rutherford (1600-1661)
The Power of Faith in Prayer

Is Christianity Hard or Easy?

The Christian way is different – harder and easier. Christ says, "Give Me all. I don't want so much of your time and so much of your money and so much of your work: I want You. I have not come to torment your natural self – but to kill it. No half measures are any good. I don't want to cut off a new branch here or there, but to have the whole tree down. I don't want to drill the tooth, or to crown it or fill it but to have it out. Hand over the whole natural self, all the desires which you think innocent, as well as the ones you think wicked – the whole outfit. I will give you a new self instead. In fact, I will give you *myself*. My own will shall become yours."

C.S. Lewis (1898-1963)
The Joyful Christian

Believing, as I do, that Jehovah is a real being, indeed the ens realissmum, I cannot sufficiently admire the divine tact of thus training the chosen races for centuries in religion before even hinting the shining secret of eternal life. He behaves like the rich lover in a romance who woos the maiden on his own merits, disguised as a poor man, and only when he has won her reveals that he has a throne and a palace to offer. For I cannot help thinking that any religion which begins with a thirst for immortality is damned, as a religion, from the outset. Until a certain spiritual level has been reached, the promise of immortality will always operate as a bribe which vitiates the whole religion and infinitely inflames those very *self regards* which religion must cut down and uproot. For the essence of religion, in my view, is the thirst for an end higher than natural ends; the finite self's desire for, and acquiescence in, and *self rejection* in favor of; an object wholly good, and wholly good for it. That the self rejection will turn out to be also a self finding, that bread cast upon the waters will be found after many days, that to die is to live – these are sacred paradoxes of which the human race must not be told too soon.

C.S. Lewis (1898-1963)
God in the Dock
Religion without Dogma

Be not cast down in heart to hear that the world barketh at Christ's strangers, both in Ireland and in this land; they do it because their Lord hath chosen them out of this world. And this is one of our Lord's reproaches –to be hated and ill treated by men. The silly stranger, in an uncouth country, must take with a smoky inn and coarse cheer, a hard bed and a barking, ill-tongued host. Indeed our fair morning is at hand, the day star is near the rising, and we are not many miles from home...what matters ill entertainment in the smoky inns of this miserable life? We are not to stay here, and we will be dearly welcome to Him whom we go to.

Samuel Rutherford (1600-1661)
Letters XXVI to Marion McNaught (1632)

And they were both naked, the man and his wife, and were not ashamed.

Genesis 2:25 KJV

Unfallen man needed no covering and asked for none; but fallen man, under the bitter consciousness of the unworthy and unseemly condition to which sin had reduced him, as unfit for God or angels, or man to look upon, cries out for covering – covering such as will hide his shame even from the eye of God. Hence He who undertook to provide this covering, must bear the shame. And He has *borne* it – all the shame of hanging naked on the cross; the shame of a sinner;, the shame of being made the song of the drunkard; the shame of being despised and rejected of men; the shame of being treated as an outcast, one unfit for either God or man to look upon, – unfit not only to live, but even to die within the gates of the holy city. All that shame He has borne for us that we might, inherit His glory.

Horatius Bonar (1808-1889)

Athasius, referring to Christ being stripped of His garments, remarks strikingly, 'It became Him when leading men *into* paradise to put off the garments which Adam received when he was cast out.' As if Christ thus took more completely our shame as well as our sin upon Him.

Horatius Bonar (1808-1889)

The Meaning of the Look

I think that look of Christ might seem to say,
"Thou Peter! Art thou then, a common stone
Which I at last must break my heart upon.
For all God's charge to His high angels may
Guard my foot better? Did I yesterday
Wash *thy* feet, my beloved, that they should run
Quick to deny me 'neath the morning sun?
And do Thy kisses, like the rest, betray?
The cock crows coldly. Hopeless, go, and manifest
A late contrition, but no bootless* fear!
For when thy final need is dreariest.
Thou shalt not be denied, as I am here:
My voice to God and angels shall attest,
"Because I KNOW *this man, let him be clear."*

Elisabeth Barrett Browning (1806-1861)

* bootless = unnecessary, useless

The Church

As to the taking of woman from the side of man

From neither extremity of Adam's body did God take the woman, signifying that she was neither to be man's lord, nor man's drudge, but his fellow, only with this inferiority, that she was taken out of Him, and therefore he was to be her head. From that part which lies nearest his heart did woman come...Not a separate being in which man could not recognize a part of himself, but a being thoroughly identified with him; not merely like him, but one with him so that her absence would be the absence of a part of himself – a blank, a void, without whom he would be incomplete.

Horatius Bonar (1808-1889)
Thoughts on Genesis

As to the making of a woman

And thus the Church, Christ's chosen Bride, springing from his smitten side, is 'builded;' – builded by the same Almighty hands that built the wondrous heavens; builded as was the temple of old, without sound of axe or hammer; builded, at once as the *City* of the Lamb's special habitation, and the *companion* for his dearest fellowship, without whom the goodly universe would have been incomplete to Him; for even in it, though renewed and glorified, it would have been found that it was 'not good for Him to be alone.' For Him no help meet could have been found, had not the Father provided this 'glorious Church' and had not He Himself, in the greatness of His longing for that help meet, consented to sleep the deep sleep of death upon the cross, that *she* might be taken out of Him, whose beauty, as seen pictured in the Father's purpose, had already 'ravished His heart' (Song 4:9) whose presence could alone make even the better paradise complete; and union to whom, throughout eternity, was what His heart desired.

Horatius Bonar (1808-1889)
Thoughts on Genesis

As Eve was taken out of the side of the first Adam as he slept; so the Church is taken out of the riven, pierced side of the second Adam as he hung in death – taken, as a Bride for Christ.

As Adam and Eve lost the Eternal *Life* of God living *in* them, with the fall. They were doomed to *die*. They hid from God. They were naked and ashamed.

To be restored to God – to be one with Him again (the two shall be one flesh), she must again be reunited with her husband, her lover, Christ, as the branch is to the vine, with the same sap (the Holy Spirit) running through her. She must be washed and born again into a new creature *in* Christ.

Horatius Bonar (1808-1889)
Thoughts on Genesis

The case in short, is this: though man is made to consist of body and soul, yet his spiritual part had then so much the dominion over his corporeal part, that he was denominated a living soul (Genesis 2:7), but by indulging the appetite of the flesh, in eating forbidden fruit, he prostituted the just domain of the soul to the tyranny of sensual lust, and became no longer a living soul, but flesh: *'Dust thou art'* ; the living soul became dead and inactive: thus in the day he sinned he 'surely died,' and so he became earthly. In this degenerate state, he begat a son in his own likeness...corruption and sin are woven into our nature; 'we are shapen in iniquity,' which makes it necessary that the nature be changed. 'You must be born again,' Christ hath said it, and as He Himself never did, nor ever will unsay it, so all the world cannot *gainsay* it, that we must be born again.

Matthew Henry (1662-1714)
Commentary on the Whole Bible
John 3:7

Chapter 4

Self

The works of the devil are all wrought in self; it is his peculiar workhouse.

William Law
The Spirit of Prayer

Self is the whole evil of fallen nature. Self is the root, the tree, and the branches of all the evils of our fallen state. Self is not only the seat and habitation, but the very life of sin.

William Law (1686-1761)
The Spirit of Prayer

The *natural* Life of the Creature was brought forth for the Participation of some high supernatural Good in the Creator. It is – in itself – both an Extremity of Need and an Extremity of Desire of some High Good.

It must covet – it is a desire proceeding from need.
It must envy – it is a desire turned to self.
It must long for power and glory – it is a desire founded on a genuine lack of exaltation to a higher state before the fall.

Wrath is born when these three are thwarted.

These 4 properties generate one another, and therefore generate their own torment. They have no outward cause nor any inward power of altering themselves.

For reason, with all its Doctrine, Discipline and Rules, can only help us to be so good, so changed, and amended, as a wild beast may be, that by restraints and methods – is taught to put on a sort of tameness, though its wild nature is all the time, only restrained and in readiness to break forth again as occasion shall offer.

Til fallen man is born again from above – Til such a supernatural birth is brought forth *in* him, by the eternal Word and Spirit of God – he can have no possible escape or deliverance from these 4 elements of self or hell.

William Law (1686-1761)
The Way to Divine Knowledge

For every temper or passion that is contrary to the new birth of Christ, and keeps the holy Immanuel from coming to life in the soul, is, in the strictest truth of the words, a murderer and killer of the Lord of Life. And where pride, and envy, and hatred, etc. are suffered to live there the same thing is done as when Christ was killed and Barabas was saved alive. The Christ of God was not then first crucified when the Jews brought Him to the cross; but Adam and Eve were His first real murderers; for the death which happened to them in the day that they did eat of the earthly tree was the death of the Christ of God, or the divine life in their souls.

William Law (1686-1761)
The Spirit of Love

I have been crucified with Christ, and it is no longer I that live, but Christ that lives in me.

Galatians 2:20 ESV

Just when we most earnestly desire to live like this, the weary old <u>self</u> seems to come to life again – the "I" that we had trusted was crucified with Christ. It is very disappointing when this happens, and the devil watches not far away, and very quietly and with great subtlety, he tries to draw us into hopeless distress and despair. If he can do that, he is satisfied, for then we are occupied with *ourselves*, which is what he wants us to be.

The one and only thing is to look straight off ourselves and our wretched failure, and cry to Him who is mighty to save. He never refuses that cry; so do not fear. The moment <u>self</u> is recognized, look to Him. Do not be discouraged; He who has begun a good work in us will go on to perfect it. The going-on may take time; even so, He will go on till (O blessed "till") we are perfected. (Philippians 1:6)

Amy Carmichael (1867-1951)
Edges of His Ways

Ye cannot serve God and mammon.

Matthew 6:24 KJV

Mammon – in a word <u>self</u> – the unity in which the world's trinity centers – sensual, secular self – is the mammon which cannot be served in conjunction with God …. He does not say "We must not or we should not, but we <u>cannot</u> love both or hold by both in observance, obedience, attendance, trust and dependence – for they are contrary the one to the other.

Matthew Henry (1662-1715)
Commentary on the Bible
Matthew 6

For the first time I examined myself with a seriously practical purpose. And there I found what appalled me; a zoo of lusts, a bedlam of ambitions, a nursery of fears, a harem of fondled hatreds. My name was legion.

C.S. Lewis (1898-1963)
Surprised by Joy: The Shape of My Early Life

Chapter 5

Sin and Satan

God's wounds cure:
Sin's kisses kill.

William Gurnall

What an astonishing thing is sin, which makes the God of Love and Father of Mercies an enemy to His creatures, and which can only be purged by the blood of the Son of God!

Thomas Adams (1701-1784)
The Treasury of David

The arrogant cannot stand in Your presence; You hate all who do wrong.

Psalm 5:5 NIV

Few are saved; men go to heaven in ones and twos, and the whole world lieth in sin.

Samuel Rutherford (1600-1661)
Letters

The earth is the portion of bastards: seek the Son's inheritance.

Samuel Rutherford (1600-1661)
Letter CXXXVI

No, young man, you may have all the vices and all the pleasure and mirth of this metropolis – and there is much to be found, of which I make no mention here – and when you have it all, you will find it does not equal your expectation, nor satisfy your desires. When the devil is bringing you one cup of spiced wine, you will be asking him next time to spice it higher; and he will flavor it to your fiery taste, but you will be dissatisfied still, until, at last, if he were to bring you a cup hot as damnation, it would fall tasteless on your palate. You would say "Even this is tasteless to me, except in the gall, and bitter wormwood, and fire that it brings." It is so with all worldly pleasures; there is no end to it; it is a perpetual thirst...even while they last, they are not wide enough for our desire, they are not large enough for our expectations, "*for the bed is shorter than a man can stretch himself on it.*" Isaiah 28:20 KJV

C.H. Spurgeon (1834-1892)
The Treasury of David

Note: The possession which the devil gets is for destruction, thus the devil hurries people to sin, hurries them to that which they have resolved against, and which they know well will be shame and grief to them: with what force doth the evil spirit work in the children of disobedience when, by so many foolish and hurtful lusts, they are brought to act in direct contradiction, not only to religion, but to right reason, and their interest in this world. Thus, likewise, he hurries them to ruin, for he is Apollyon and Abbaddon, the great destroyer. By his lusts which men do, they are drowned in destruction and perdition. This is Satan's will – to swallow up and devour; miserable then is the condition of those that are led captive by him at his will.

Matthew Henry (1662-1714)
Commentary on the Bible
Matthew 8:32

I tell you the truth – everyone who sins is a slave to sin. Now a slave has no permanent place in the family, but a son belongs to it forever –

So if the Son sets you free, you will be free indeed.

John 8:34-35 NIV

The reason the Son of God appeared was to destroy the devil's work.

1 John 3:8 NIV

———————————————

Do not be anxious about anything…..

Philippians 4:6 NIV

There is scarcely any one sin against which our Lord Jesus more largely and earnestly warns His disciples – or against which He arms them with more variety of arguments - than the sin of disquieting, distracting, distrustful cares about the things of life, which are a bad sign that both the treasure and the heart are on the earth.

Matthew Henry (1662-1714)
Commentary

———————————————

…A triumph when temptation's bribe
Is slowly handed back,
One eye upon the heaven renounced
And one upon the rack…

Emily Dickinson (1830-1886)

Saul and Judas each said "I have sinned;" but David says, "I have sinned against Thee."

William S. Plummer
Psalm 41:4 KJV
The Treasury of David

He shows that there is no little sin, because there is no little God to sin against.

Matthew Henry (1662-1714)
Commentary

Holy Scripture – when it depicts God's wrath against sin – never uses an hyperbole: it would be impossible to exaggerate it.

C.H. Spurgeon (1834-1892)
The Treasury of David
Psalm 90:11

A single sin clinging to you will make you stand still in your progress.

Andrew Bonar (1810-1892)
Heavenly Springs

My dear friend must not go in search of his own wretchedness; enough of it will be apparent when God sees fit. Let not your depravity be the chief object of your thoughts. God, as your friend and Savior, God, as present in your heart, ought to be that object. And when you are obliged to see and feel your corruptions, endure it in the presence of God, just as a sick child upon its mother's lap, causes the pain it feels, to be understood, only by the moving expression of its eyes. The view of ourselves disorders us; our cure is in looking unto God.

Gerhard Tersteegen (1697-1769)
Life and Writings

He that does not believe that there is a God, is more vile than a devil. To deny that there is a god, is the sort of atheism that is not to be found in hell.

Thomas Brooks

And he [Satan] said to the woman, can it really be that God has said......

Genesis 3:1 Amplified

A single question is put. God's character is maligned. The lie is believed. Man suspects God and perishes! Such is the dark process still by which Satan thinks to hinder our return to God. His aim is to misrepresent God to man; to prove God to be unkind in what He has prohibited, and a liar in what He has declared.

Horatius Bonar (1808-1889)

...she gave me some fruit and I ate it!

Genesis 3:12 Amplified

...To own himself totally a sinner – made so, not by God, not by any fellow-creature, nor by education, not by circumstances, but solely by himself, is what he will not stoop to. Yet on any other terms God cannot deal with him. As a confessed sinner, he may at any moment go to God, assured of finding favor and pardon; but on any other footing, approach to God must be wholly in vain...Nor will terror ever do anything but drive a man from God. Nothing but grace can do this...Terror drives men into the thicket, only grace can draw him out.

Horatius Bonar (1808-1889)

She also gave some to her husband, who was with her.

Genesis 3:6 KJV

The tendency of sin to propagate itself; no sooner has the tempted one yielded than he seeks to draw others into the snare. He must drag down his fellows with him. There seems an awful vitality about sin; a fertility in reproduction, nay, a horrid necessity of nature for self-diffusion. It never lies dormant.

Horatius Bonar (1808-1889)
Thoughts on Genesis

Sorrow wells out of sin just as blood wells out of a wound.

Andrew Bonar (1810-1892)

There is a natural tendency in sin to destruction.

Matthew Henry (1662-1714)
Commentary Proverbs 1

Adam's sin drew down on the soil the curse of fruitfulness in evil. (Gen 3:3) Cain's draws down on it the curse of barrenness in good....It was to afford him no settled dwelling...he was to become a wanderer over earth; his sin, like a malignant demon, pursuing him, and allowing him no rest for the sole of his foot. As Israel, in after days, were made wanderers among the nations for the blood shedding of the Lord of glory, so was Cain...such is sin! So terrible, so ruinous, so relentless, so armed with the curse of God. Such are the fruits of envy. Burden upon burden stroke upon stroke, sorrow upon sorrow! From above, from beneath, and from around, the torment, and the terror, and the bitterness pour in. There is no peace for the wicked, no rest, no settlement.

Horatius Bonar (1808-1889)
Thoughts on Genesis

Cain's Sin – Remorse

Like Judas, he is stung with remorse as when the betrayer cried out, "I have sinned, in that I have betrayed the innocent blood." He now, for the first time, confesses sin; yet it is only this sin – no more – that he avows...for there is no right sense of sin here, but the mere agony of blind remorse, arising from the reaction and revulsion of his furious passions, and the terrible thought that he is in the hands of an angry God....Remorse is not repentance. Terror is not repentance. Despair is not repentance. The revenge which an outraged conscience takes on man for some dark deed is not repentance. These are but Cain's sullen ravings, or Ahab's alarm, or Judas' despair. There are outcries such as these in hell, with weeping and wailing and gnashing of teeth; but where is godly sorrow, the tears of a broken heart?

Horatius Bonar (1808-1889)
Thoughts on Genesis

True repentance strikes at the darling sin, and will – with a peculiar zeal and resolution, put away that – the sin which most *easily besets us.*

Matthew Henry (1662-1714)
1 Samuel 7:3

Remorse

Remorse is memory awake,
Her companies astir –
A presence of departed acts
At window and at door.

It's past set down before the soul,
And lighted with a match,
Perusal to facilitate
Of its condensed dispatch.

Remorse is cureless – the disease
Not even God can heal;
For 'tis his institution
The compliment of hell.

Emily Dickinson (1830-1886)

Sin is the Trojan horse that lands an army of afflictions upon us.

Thomas Watson (1620-1686)
The Lord's Prayer

When a servant of God meets these sins in others, let him be reverent with what He does not understand and leave God to deal with them.

Certain forms of sin shock us far more than they shock God.

Oswald Chambers (1874-1917)
Conformed to His Image

Are we so noisy in our instruction of other people that God cannot get near them?

Oswald Chambers (1874-1917)
My Utmost for His Highest

Satan is an angry and discontented spirit. He finds no rest but in restless hearts.

John Flavel (1627-1691)
Keeping the Heart

If Satan have half, he will have all.

Matthew Henry (1662-1714)
Commentary

They banded themselves against the Lord, and against His Anointed...They had the devils' mind, which is not satisfied but with death.

Henry Smith
The Treasury of David

God always comes unseasonably to a carnal heart. It was the devil that said, *"Art thou come hither to torment us before the time?"*

The Treasury of David

God puts away many in anger for their supposed goodness, but not any at all for their confessed badness.

John Trapp
The Treasury of David
Psalm 27:9

But in this dark story (of our fallen world), there is a twofoldness, a duality throughout, which strikes us with a strange awe. It is not two sins or two sinners that are presented to us, but two kinds of sin and two kinds of sinners; one visible, the other invisible; one human, the other superhuman; the two acting mysteriously together, yet without open compact; the invisible and the superhuman operating upon the visible and the human, and both together working against God.

Horatius Bonar (1808-1889)
Thoughts on Genesis

'No God' and 'no devil' generally go together.

Horatius Bonar (1808-1889)

...but it will scarcely be believed, that even Satan should not only have aimed so high as to supplant the adorable and eternal God as the object of Human worship, but should also have aspired to put himself forth as the object of supreme worship, and challenge the adoration of the world under the precise form in which he had succeeded in affecting the ruin of the race. Yet so it was. The serpent form has, in all probability, approached nearer to universal adoration than any other.

Mr. Smith
The Gentile Nations
Thoughts on Genesis by Horatius Bonar

.... So He got up from the meal, took off His outer clothing, and wrapped a towel around His waist. After that He poured water into a basin and began to wash His disciples feet.....

John 13:4-5 NIV

Sins are obvious things, but perhaps the dust on the feet means things less easily discerned. That inward uprising of the "I", these lacks of which we are conscious more and more – lacks of love, courage, patience, simple good-tempered contentedness – such lack make dusty feet.

Is it not blessed and wonderful that He himself prepared the disciples for the Supper? We may not see the dust distinctly, but He does, and He poured water into a basin, and began to wash the disciples' feet...when we remember our dear Lord's death, is it not peace to know that He Himself will prepare us?

Amy Carmichael (1867-1951)
Whispers of His Power

To conclude with a word to the wicked, who march furiously against God and His people – let them know that God's decree is unchangeable. God will not alter it, nor can they break it – and while they resist God's will, they fulfill it. There is a two-fold will of God – the will of God's precept and of His decree. While the wicked resist the will of God's precept, they fulfill the will of His permissive decree...Judas betrays Christ – Pilate condemns Him, the soldiers crucify Him...so while men break the silken net of God's command they are taken in the iron net of His decree; while they sit backwards to God's precepts, they row forward to His decrees; His decrees to permit their sin – and to *punish* them for their sin permitted.

Thomas Watson (1620-1686)
A Body of Divinity

Chapter 6

Death to Self

Die before you die.
There is no chance after that.

C.S.Lewis
'Til We Have Faces

Then I saw a Lamb, looking as if it had been slain.

Revelation 5:6 NIV

But why life taken? Why "death" required? Because the essence of sin is an attack on God's holy throne and His very existence. It is, therefore, repelled by God crushing the sinner's life. And Jesus bore even this for men! *"Ye have slain the Prince of Life!"*

Andrew Bonar (1810-1892)
Leviticus

Opening our windows toward Jerusalem
And looking thitherward, we see
First Bethlehem,
Then Nazareth and Galilee,
And afterwards Gethsemane;
And then the little hill called Calvary.

Amy Carmichael (1867-1951)
Toward Jerusalem

Know ye not, that so many of us as were baptized into Jesus Christ were baptized into His death? ...Likewise reckon ye also yourselves to be dead indeed unto sin, but alive unto God through Jesus Christ, our Lord.

Romans 6:3, 11 KJV

There is something in this universe which is the very opposite of God; it is the self. The activity of the self is the source of all the evil nature as well as all the evil deeds of men. On the other hand – the loss of the selfhood in the soul increases the purity of the soul; in fact, the soul's purity is increased in exact proportion to the loss of self.

Madame Guyon (1648 -1717)

We who are alive are always being given over to death, for Jesus' sake, so that His life may be revealed in our mortal body.

2 Corinthians 4:11 NIV

And Yet

Have I been so long time with thee
And yet hast thou not known Me?

Blesséd Master, I have known Thee
On the roads of Galilee.

Have I been so long time with Thee
on the roads of Galilee:

Yet, my child, hast thou not known Me
when I walked upon the sea?

Blesséd Master, I have known Thee
On the roads and on the sea.

Wherefore then hast thou not known Me
Broken in Gethsemane?

I would have thee follow, know Me
Thorn-crowned, nailed upon the Tree.

Canst thou follow, wilt thou know Me
All the way to Calvary?

Amy Carmichael (1867-1951)
Toward Jerusalem

In every Christian's heart there is a cross and a throne, and the Christian is on the throne 'til he puts himself on the cross; if he refuses the cross he remains on the throne. Perhaps this is at the bottom of the backsliding and worldliness among gospel believers today. We want to be saved but we insist that Christ do all the dying.

A.W. Tozer (1897-1963)
The Root of Righteousness

Let no man take fright at Christ – for I have no quarrels at His cross – He and His cross are two good guests and well worth the lodging. Men would fain have Christ good cheap; (on sale) but the market will not come down.

Samuel Rutherford (1600-1661)
Letter CXXII

Oh, how sweet are the sufferings of Christ for Christ! God forgive them that raise an ill report upon the sweet cross of Christ. It is but our weak and dim eyes, and our looking only to the black side that makes us mistake. Those who can take that crabbed tree handsomely upon their back, and fasten it on cannily, shall find it such a burden as wings unto a bird, or sails to a ship.

Samuel Rutherford (1600-1661)
Letter LXIX

The one true way of dying to self is most simple and plain – it wants no arts or methods, no cells, monasteries or pilgrimages – it is equally practical by everybody – it is always at hand – it meets you in everything – it is free from all deceit – it never meets *without success.*

If you ask what this one, true, simple, plain, immediate, and unerring way is – it is the way of patience, meekness, humility, and resignation to God. This is the truth and perfection of dying to self – it is nowhere else, nor possible to be in anything else – but in this state of heart.

William Law (1686-1761)
The Spirit of Love

Thus doth the soul ascend unto God, by giving up self to the destroying and annihilation power of Divine Love; this, indeed, is a most essential and necessary sacrifice in the Christian religion, and that alone by which we pay true homage to the sovereignty of God.

Madame Guyon (1648-1717)
A Short Method of Prayer

Search and look where you will, this Denial of Self is the one only possible way to the Truth. For nothing has separated us from Truth, nothing stands betwixt us and Truth, but this Self of an earthly life, which is not from God, but from our wandering out of our first created state.

William Law (1686-1761)
The Way to Divine Knowledge

...instead of showing the Reasonableness of believing a long History of things, show the absolute Necessity of man's dying to his present life, in order to have a better from God.

William Law (1686-1761)
The Way to Divine Knowledge

Here is a true spiritual principle that the Lord will not deny: God gives us the cross, and then the cross gives us God.

Madam Guyon (1648-1717)
Experiencing the Depths of Jesus Christ

Humility is the blossom, of which death to self is the perfect fruit.

Andrew Murray (1828-1917)
Humility

For we who are alive are always being given over to death for Jesus' sake, so that His life may be revealed in our mortal body.

2 Corinthians 4:11 NIV

Here is a trustworthy saying: If we died with Him, we will also live with Him.

2 Timothy 2:11 NIV

I have been crucified with Christ and I no longer live, but Christ lives in me.

Galatians 2:20 NIV

If there were any one among men immortal, not liable to sin, or change – whom it were impossible for anyone to overcome – but who was as strong as an angel – such a one might *be* something. But insomuch as everyone is a man, a sinner, mortal, weak, liable to sickness and death – exposed to pain and terror, like Pharaoh – even from the most insignificant animals- and liable to so many miseries that it is impossible to count them – the conclusion must be a valid one – "Man is nothing."

The Treasury of David
Psalm 62:9

Nevertheless, if you are fully convinced that it is on the nothing in man that God establishes His greatest works, you will be in part, guarded against disappointment or surprise. He destroys that He might build – for when He is about to rear His sacred temple in us, He first totally razes that vain and pompous edifice, which human art and power had erected – and from its horrible ruins, a new structure is formed – by His power only.

Madame Guyon (1648-1717)
The Autobiography

Abandonment

Abandonment is the casting off all selfish care that we may be altogether at the divine disposal...our abandonment then should be, both in respect to external and internal things, an absolute giving up of all our concerns into the hands of God, forgetting ourselves and thinking only of Him, by which the heart will remain always disengaged, free and at peace.

It is practiced by continually losing our own will in the will of God, renouncing every private inclination as soon as it arises, however good it may appear, that we may stand in indifference with respect to ourselves and only will what God has willed from all eternity, resigning ourselves in all things, whether for soul or body, from time or eternity, forgetting the past, leaving the future to Providence, and devoting the present to God, satisfied with the present moment, which brings with it God's eternal order in reference to us, and is as infallible a declaration of His will, as it is inevitable and common to all, attributing nothing that befalls us to the creature but regarding all things in God, and looking upon all, excepting only our sins, as infallibly proceeding from Him.

Surrender yourselves then to be led and disposed of just as God pleases, with respect both to your outward and inward state.

Be patient under all the sufferings God sends. If your love to Him be pure, you will not seek Him less on Calvary, than on Tabor, and surely He should be as much loved on that as on this, since it was on Calvary that He made the greatest display of love. Be not like those who give themselves to Him at one season, only to withdraw from Him at another. They give themselves only to be caressed, and wrest themselves back again, when they are crucified or at least turn for consolation to the creature.

Madame Guyon (1648-1717)
Experiencing the Depths of Jesus Christ

The Sign

Lord crucified, O mark Thy holy cross
On motive, preference, all fond desires;
On that which self in any form inspires
Set Thou that sign of loss.

And when the touch of death is here and there
Laid on a thing most precious in our eyes,
Let us not wonder, let us recognize
The answer to this prayer.

Amy Carmichael (1867-1951)
Toward Jerusalem

There are others, who, being called of God to die to themselves, yet pass all their time in a dying life – in inward agonies – without ever entering into God through death and a total loss of self – because they are always willing to retain something – under plausible pretexts – and so never lose themselves to the whole extent of the designs of God.

Madame Guyon (1648-1717)

Jesus' primary consideration is my absolute annihilation of my right to myself and my identification with Him – which means having a relationship with Him in which there are no other relationships.

Oswald Chambers (1874-1917)
My Utmost for His Highest
(Updated Edition)

Therefore, I urge you, brothers, in view of God's mercy to offer your bodies as living sacrifices holy and pleasing to God.

Romans 12:1 NIV

"If anyone would come after Me, he must deny himself and take up his cross daily and follow Me. For whoever wants to save his life will lose it, but whoever loses his life for Me will save it.

Luke 9:23-24 NIV

There are but these two truths – the All and the Nothing; everything else is a falsehood. We pay honor to the All of God, only in our own Annihilation, which, He, who never suffers a void in nature, instantly fills us with Himself.

Madame Guyon (1648-1717)
Autobiography

This speaks of something far more than mere abandonment of one's material possessions; it is an absolute, unconditional surrender. The disciples were permitted to retain no privileges and make no demands. They were to safeguard no cherished sins, treasure no earthly possessions, and cling to no secret self-indulgence. Their commitment to Him must be without reservation.

John MacArthur Study Bible – footnote p. 1545

The one principle of hell is "I am my own."

George Macdonald

For no sin is more abominable to God than pride.

Matthew Henry (1662-1714)
Commentary on Isaiah 4

How very straight is the gate which leads to life in God! How little one must be to pass through it – it being nothing else but death to self.

Madame Guyon (1648-1717)
Autobiography

The only way is by allowing nothing of the old life to remain; and by having only simple perfect trust in God – such a trust that we no longer want God's blessings, but only want God Himself.

Oswald Chambers (1874-1917)
My Utmost for His Highest

No Scar?

Hast thou no scar?
No hidden scar on foot, or side, or hand?
I hear thee sung as mighty in the land,
I hear them hail thy bright ascendant star,
Hast thou no scar?

Hast thou no wound?
Yet I was wounded by the archers, spent,
Leaned Me against a tree to die; and rent
By ravening beasts that compassed Me, I swooned:
Hast thou no scar no wound?

No wound? No scar?
Yet, as the Master shall the servant be,
And piercéd are the feet that follow Me;
But thine are whole: can he have followed far
Who has nor wound nor scar?

Amy Carmichael (1867-1951)
Toward Jerusalem

All our strength, peace and salvation must be sought in this inwardly abiding – with a childlike spirit – *in* Jesus...Let us then remain resigned to Him, with an introverted eye, and boldly pursue our course – forsaking all we are – that Jesus alone, may possess and rule *in* us. O my dear brethren, let us forsake ourselves! In us there is nothing but perdition, misery and weakness. *In* Jesus there is real life and salvation. Let everyone seek and experience it for himself. We must be found actively *in* Him.

Gerhard Tersteegen (1697-1769)
Life and Writings

We then enjoy all things whilst desiring nothing...but you know as well as I that the Spirit of Jesus can *alone* impart true resignation and every other fundamental virtue. The pure influence of this lively power, which is so exceedingly near us, is *alone* able to destroy self, and soften and allay the ardent fire of nature, so that we run with patience, and sit still without being idle because in the manner, Christ Himself becomes our will, our life and our delight. How happy therefore are those souls, who walk in the way of the heart, and silently retire within themselves – waiting, praying, and giving place to the operation of Him who alone giveth life.

Gerhard Tersteegen (1697-1769)
Letters

Such [practices] have indeed the outward appearance [that popularly passes] for wisdom, in promoting self-imposed rigor of devotion, and delight in self-humiliation and severity of discipline of the body, but they are of no value in checking the indulgence of the flesh (the lower nature). [Instead, they do not honor God, but serve only to indulge the flesh.]

Colossians 2:23
Amplified Bible

It is of great importance to guard against vexation on account of our faults; it springs from a secret root of pride and a love of our own excellence; we are hurt at feeling what we are.

Madame Guyon (1648-1717)
Experiencing the Depths of Jesus Christ

Not to be occupied with thy sin, but to be occupied with God, brings deliverance from self.

Andrew Murray (1828-1917)

...and this He does to prevent the damage that would be done to them by the pomp and vainglory of this wretched life, and to prepare their path to heaven, and to raise them to His bliss which lasts without end; for He says, "I shall shatter you for your vain passions and your vicious pride, and after that I shall gather you together and make you humble and meek, pure and holy, by uniting you to Me.

Julian of Norwich (1342-1416)
Long Text

To the graceless neck, the yoke of Christ is intolerable, but to the saved sinner, it is easy and light...we may judge ourselves by this – do we love that yoke, or do we wish to cast it from us?

C.H. Spurgeon (1834-1892)

But his delight is in the law of the Lord, and on His law he meditates day and night. He is like a tree planted by streams of water, which yields its fruit in season and whose leaf does not wither.

Psalm 1:2-3 NIV

Well, if in truth God is ready to give, not just a little, but lavishly, whatever we need for victorious life, then it follows that we need not fail. When we fail it must be that we have put some barriers between ourselves and our supply. I think it is here that we need to direct prayer- prayer against barriers – and these are nearly always made of self-love in one form or another. God save us from that, and enable us to receive that which He so lavishly gives.

Amy Carmichael (1867-1951)
Edges of His Ways

Man or Rabbit?

We are to be remade. All the rabbit in us is to disappear – the worried, conscientious, ethical rabbit as well as the cowardly and sensual rabbit. We shall bleed and squeal as the handfuls of fur come out; and then surprisingly, we shall find underneath it all a thing we have never yet imagined – a real Man, an ageless God and son of God, strong, radiant, wise, beautiful, and drenched in joy.

C.S. Lewis (1898-1963)
God in the Dock

Chapter 7

Thy Will Be Done

One read tomes on the work of the Holy Spirit – when five minutes of drastic obedience would make things clear as a sunbeam.

Oswald Chambers
Complete Works

You need to persevere so that when you have done the will of God, you will receive what He has promised.

Hebrews 10:36 NIV

This verse made me think of how continually our Lord makes obedience the test of love: *"He that hath My commandments, and keepeth them, he it is who loveth Me."* I was thinking, too, of how each act of obedience opens a window in Heaven, and light pours through upon the soul that obeys, and it walks on in that Heavenly light; whereas, just as certainly, the least disobedience shuts the window. No more light comes through....If I disobey, it must be because I love someone else more. Who?

Amy Carmichael (1867-1951)
Edges of His Ways

As servants take their cue from the master's eye, and a nod or a wink is all they require, so should we obey the slightest hints of our Master, not needing thunderbolts to startle our incorrigible sluggishness, but being controlled by whispers and love touches.

C.H. Spurgeon (1834-1892)
Psalm 32:8
The Treasury of David

For the new world into which we pass is the world of God's sovereign will – where the will of man cannot come – or if it comes, it is as a dependent and a servant, never as a Lord.

A.W. Tozer (1897-1963)
God's Pursuit of Man

There is such a thing as shining contentment with the will of God. Any lack there is a loss to prayer.

Amy Carmichel (1867-1951)
Whispers of His Power

May we give up our will to Thine, and feel as if a burden were lifted off us and laid on Thee.

Andrew Bonar (1810-1892)
Heavenly Springs

Good works do not make a good man, but a good man does good works.

Martin Luther (1483-1546)
Great Voices of the Reformation

———————————

The Lord will not save them whom He cannot command. Christ must be Lord or He will not be Savior.

A.W. Tozer (1897-1963)
The Root of the Righteousness

———————————

I lost not Thy presence, which was given me by a continual infusion, not as I had imagined, by the efforts of the head, or by force of thought in meditating on God, but in the <u>will</u>, where I tasted with unutterable sweetness the enjoyment of the Beloved object. In a happy experience I knew that the soul was created to enjoy its God.

The union of the will subjects the soul to God, conforms it to all His pleasure, <u>causes self-will gradually to die.</u> Lastly, in drawing with it the other powers, by means of the charity with which it is filled, it causes them gradually to be reunited in the center and lost there as to their own nature and operation.

Madame Guyon (1648-1717)

Surrender is not the surrender of the external life, but of the will; and when that is done, all is done.

Oswald Chambers (1874-1917)
My Utmost for His Highest

Revelation is the first step to holiness, and consecration is the second. A day must come in our lives, as definite as the day of our conversion, when we give up all right to ourselves and submit to the absolute Lordship of Jesus Christ. There may be a practical issue raised by God to test the reality of our consecration, but whether that be so or not, there must be a day when, without reservation, we surrender everything to Him – ourselves, our possessions, our business and our time. All we are, and all we have becomes His, to be held henceforth entirely at His disposal. From that day we are no longer our own masters, but only stewards. Not until the Lordship of Jesus Christ is a settled thing in our hearts, can the Spirit really operate effectively in us....If we do not give Him absolute authority in our lives, He can be present, but He cannot be powerful. The power of the Spirit if stayed.

Watchman Nee (1903-1972)
The Normal Christian Life

Free will is a weather cock turning at a serpent's tongue, a tutor that cowped (upset, overturned) our Father Adam, unto us; and brought down the house, and sold the land, and sent the father and mother, and all the bairns (children) through the earth to beg their bread.

Samuel Rutherford (1600-1661)
Letter CXX

There is nothing so gentle as the check of the Holy Spirit.

Oswald Chambers (1874-1917)
Conformed to His Image

Notice how in your own life He works. He begins with the big general principles and then slowly educates you down to the scruple.

Oswald Chambers (1874-1917)
Conformed to His Image

Our absolute surrender of ourselves to the Lord generally hinges upon some one particular thing, and God is after that one thing. He must have it for He must have our all....He is not calling us to devote ourselves to His cause: He is asking us to yield ourselves to His <u>will</u>. Are you willing for anything He wills? ... A forgiven sinner is quite different from an ordinary sinner, and a consecrated Christian is quite different from an ordinary Christian.

Watchman Nee (1903-1972)
The Normal Christian Life

It is altogether doubtful whether any man can be saved who comes to Christ for His help, but with no intention to obey Him.

A.W. Tozer (1897-1963)
The Root of the Righteous

When the soul is docile, and leaves itself to be purified, and emptied of all that, which it has of its own – opposite to the will of God – it finds itself, little by little, detached from every emotion of its own, and placed in a holy indifference, wishing nothing but what God does and wills.

Madame Guyon (1648-1717)
The Autobiography

...whoever loses his life for my sake will find it.

Matthew 10:39 NIV

The world must learn that I love the Father and that I do exactly what my Father has commanded Me.

John 14:31 NIV

We know that we have come to know Him if we obey His commands.

1 John 2:3 NIV

May He remember all your sacrifices and accept your burnt offerings.

Psalm 20:3 NIV

If you want to be one of those of whom the Lord can ask anything in the days to come, begin now by laying your little offerings upon His altar. Lay down your little choices, your *will* about very little things. He will not call these love offerings little. He will accept them, and cause His face to shine upon you, and give you peace.

Amy Carmichael (1867-1951)
Thou Givest – They Gather

My food is to do the will of Him who sent Me and to finish His work.

John 4:34 NIV

For I have come down from heaven <u>not to do My own will</u>, but to do the will of Him who sent Me.

John 6:38 NIV

I had a perfect indifference to everything that is here, a union so great with the will of God that my own will seemed entirely lost. My soul could not incline itself on one side or the other, since another will had taken the place of its own, but only nourished itself with the daily providences of God. It now found a will all divine, yet was so natural and easy that it found itself infinitely more free than ever it had been on its own.

Madame Guyon (1648-1717)
The Autobiography

The surest method of arriving at a knowledge of God's eternal purposes about us, is to be found in the right use of the present moment. Each hour comes with some little fagot* of God's will fastened upon its back.

F.W. Faber
At Dawn of Day

* fagot – a little bundle of sticks for firewood

I knew Jesus and He was very precious to my soul; but I found something in me that would not keep sweet and patient and kind. I did what I could to keep it down, but it was there. I besought Jesus to do something for me, and *then I gave Him my will*, He came to my heart, and took out all that would not be sweet, all that would not be kind, and all that would not be patient – and then He shut the door.

George Fox (1624-1691)
Founder of the Quakers

Not everyone who says 'Lord, Lord' will enter the Kingdom of Heaven, but only he who does the will of my Father who is in Heaven.

Matthew 7:21 NIV

Whoever serves Me must follow Me; and where I am the servant also will be.

John 12:26 NIV

And you shall know that I am the Lord.

Ezekiel 6:7 NKJ

This clause refers 63 times in the book. It shows that the essential reason for judgement is the violation of the character of God...the motive for all obedience to God's law is the fact that *He is the Lord God.*

John MacArthur
Study Bible

———————————————————

I was afraid of not doing His will by being too ardent and hasty in doing it.

Madame Guyon (1648-1717)
Autobiography

The way of inward peace – is in all things, to be conformed to the pleasure and disposition of the Divine Will. Such as would have all things succeed and come to pass according to their <u>own</u> fancy, are not come to know this way – and therefore lead a harsh and bitter life – always restless and out of humor, without treading in the way of peace – which consists in a total conformity to the will of God.

Miguel de Molines (1640-1697)
A Spiritual Guide

Let's God's truth work in you by soaking in it, not by worrying into it....Obey God in the thing He shows you, and instantly the next thing is opened up.

Oswald Chambers (1874-1917)
My Utmost for His Highest

A person is simply a slave for obeying unless behind his obedience is the recognition of a holy God. Many people begin coming to God once they stop being religious, because there is only one master of the human heart – Jesus Christ, not religion. But "woe is me" if after seeing Him, I still will not obey. (Isa. 6:5)

Oswald Chambers (1874-1917)
Complete Works

Do not merely listen to the word, and so deceive yourselves. Do what it says….but the man who looks intently into the perfect law that gives freedom, and continues to do this, not forgetting what he has heard, but <u>doing</u> it – he will be blessed in what he does.

James 1:22, 25 NIV

…This is a rule without an exception. God is good to those that be good. Mercy and faithfulness shall abound toward those who through mercy are made faithful. Whatever outward appearances may threaten, we should settle it steadfastly in our minds that while grace enables us to <u>obey the Lord's will</u> we need not fear that Providence will cause us any real loss. There shall be mercy in every unsavory morsel, and faithfulness in every bitterdrop; let not our hearts be troubled, but let us rest by faith in the immutable covenant of Jehovah, which is ordered in all things and sure. Yet this is not a general truth to be trampled upon by swine; it is a pearl for a child's neck.

C.H. Spurgeon (1834-1892)
The Treasury of David

If we have a purpose of our own, it destroys the simplicity and the leisureliness which ought to characterize the children of God.

Oswald Chambers (1874-1917)
My Utmost for His Highest

If God be infinite in power, let us take heed of hardening our hearts against Him. *Who hath hardened himself against Him and prospered?* (Job 9:4) ...for a person to on daringly in any sin is to harden his heart against God, and to raise a war against heaven...such as will not bow to His golden sceptre shall be broken with His iron rod...will folly contend with wisdom; weakness with power; finite with infinite? O take heed of hardening your heart against God! He can send legions of angels to avenge His quarrel. It is better to meet God with tears in your eyes than weapons in your hand. You may overcome Him sooner by repentance than by resistance.

Thomas Watson (1620-1686)
A Body of Divinity
The Power of God

If any man will come after Me, or be My disciples, let him deny himself, and take up his cross daily and follow me.

Luke 9:23 KJV

Your "cross" is where *your* will and God's will cross.

Derek Prince

...after the sudden loss of her teacher, her mentor, and her greatly loved leader in missionary work, kind people, wanting to console, made the usual observations "It is very hard to see how this can be for the best."

"We are not asked to *see,* said Amy. Why need we when we know?

We know, not the answer to the inevitable *Why*, but the incontestable *fact* that it is for the best. It is an irreparable loss, but is it faith at all if it is hard to trust when things are entirely bewildering?

There is only one way of victory over the bitterness and rage that come naturally to us – to will what God wills brings peace. "

Elizabeth Elliot
A Chance to Die
A biography of Amy Carmichael

There may be real submission to the will of God while we can't help wishing things were otherwise. God does not ask us to *feel* that everything is for the best, but He does ask us to believe it.

Andrew Bonar (1810-1892)
Heavenly Springs

That which comes nearest and dearest of all – unhindered communion with our God – is based on His will, accepted and obeyed.

Amy Carmichael (1867-1951)
Edges of His Ways

Whenever I meet with the will of God, I feel that I meet with God. Whenever I respect and love the will of God, I feel that I respect and love God. Whenever I unite with the will of God, I feel that I unite with God; so that practically and religiously – although I am aware that a difference can be made philosophically – *God and the will of God are to me the same.* He who is in perfect harmony with the will of God, is as much in harmony with God Himself as it is possible for any being to be. The very name of God's will fills me with joy.

Madame Guyon (1648-1717)
Autobiography

A wish is a command to one who loves.

Amy Carmichael (1867-1951)

God has created the sun and the moon and the stars, and the flowers and the trees and the grass; and are they not all absolutely surrendered to God? Do they not allow God to work in them just what He pleases?

...And God's redeemed children – oh, can you think that God can work if there is only half or a part of them surrendered?

Andrew Murray (1828-1917)
Absolute Surrender

When I was in my apartment, without any other director than our Lord, by His Spirit, - as soon as one of my little children (novice nuns) came to knock at my door – He required me to admit the interruption. He showed me that it not the actions in themselves, which please Him, but the constant ready obedience to every discovery of His will, even in the minutest things, with such a suppleness as not to stick to anything, but still to turn with Him at every call. My soul was then, I thought, like a leaf or a feather, which the wind moves whatsoever way it pleases – and the Lord never suffers a soul so dependent upon and dedicated to Him to be deceived.

Madame Guyon (1648-1717)
Autobiography

Chapter 8

Loving God

"Leave her alone," said Jesus. "Why are you bothering her? She has done a beautiful thing to Me."

Mark 14:6 NIV

Have I ever produced in the heart of the Lord Jesus what Mary of Bethany produced?

Oswald Chambers
My Utmost for His Highest

Teach me to love Thee as Thine angels love,
One holy passion filling all my frame.

George Croly
Systematic Theology
Wayne Grudem (1948 -)

Thou Shall Love Thy God

A lack of love indicates that one is spiritually dead. Love is the sure test of whether someone has experienced the new birth or is still in the darkness of spiritual death.

The John MacArthur Study Bible
1 John 3:14

We know and rely on the love God has for us. God is love. Whoever lives in love, lives in God, and God in him.

1 John 4:16 NIV

Divine Love

Self love thinks 'what can I do better than to be in heaven ' and will not buy it too dear; but divine love does not regard such a heaven; the good pleasure of God is its heaven – its honor, its glory. It is this, strictly speaking, to which divine love – in its nature and properties – has respect; and the holy ambition of this love – softly, yet powerfully impels it continually, to seek more and more to please God – nor is it conscious of a greater honor or happiness – in time or eternity, than to please Him, whether at home or in the body.

Gerhard Tersteegen (1697-1769)
Life and Character

I desire to do Your will, O my God;
Your law is within my heart.

Psalm 40:8 NIV

...they should choose to set at nothing everything that is made so as to have the love of God who is unmade. This is why those who choose to occupy themselves with earthly business and are always pursuing worldly success, have nothing here of God in their hearts and souls; because they love and seek their rest in this little thing where there is no rest, and know nothing of God who is almighty – all wise and all good, for He is true rest.

Julian of Norwich (1342-1416)
Revelations of Divine Love
Short text

Take My yoke upon you and learn from Me for I am gentle and humble in heart, and you will find rest for your souls.

Matthew 11:29 NIV

***

If a sudden jar can cause me to speak an impatient, unloving word, then I know nothing of Calvary love...for a cup brimful of sweet water cannot spill even one drop of bitter water however suddenly jolted.

Amy Carmichael (1867-1951)
If

If I am inconsiderate about the comfort of others, or their feelings, or even of their little weaknesses; if I am careless about their little hurts and miss opportunities to smooth their way; if I make the sweet running of household wheels more difficult to accomplish, then I know nothing of Calvary love.

Amy Carmichael (1867-1951)
If

———

This is the end of all true "doing to death" – the end is life, not death; the life of uttermost love, love that cannot help loving anymore than the sun can help shining, or the river flowing, or the trees putting forth green leaves.

The bond that holds God's children together is love – just love. One unkind deed, one unkind word, one thought even, that moves towards unkindness, is fatal to the quality of love we must have if His love is to be *in* us. It is not a little thing to love like this, Lord, evermore give us this love.

Amy Carmichael (1867-1951)
The Edges of His Ways

As for what passes in me at present, I cannot express it. I have no pain or difficulty about my state, because I have no will but that of God – which I endeavor to accomplish in all things – and to which I am so resigned, that I would not take up a straw from the ground against His order or from any other motive but purely that of love to Him.

Brother Lawrence (1614-1691)
The Practice of the Presence of God
Second Letter

That we ought not to be weary of doing little things for the love of God, Who regards not the greatness of the work, but the love with which it is performed...that the most excellent method he had found of going to God was that of doing our common business without any view of pleasing men and, as far as we are capable, purely for the love of God.

Brother Lawrence (1614-1691)
The Practice of the Presence of God
Fourth Conversation

"Love," says St. Augustine, "and then do what you please." For when we truly love, we can't have so much as a will to do anything that might offend the object of our affections.

Madame Guyon (1648-1717)
Experiencing the Depths of Jesus Christ

I would be farther in upon Christ than at His joys; in, where love and mercy lodgeth, beside His heart. He who sitteth on the throne is alone a sufficient heaven.

Samuel Rutherford (1600-1661)
Letters

I know that for the right practice of it (the presence of God) the heart must be empty of all other things; because God will possess the heart *alone*, and as He cannot possess it alone without emptying it of all besides, so neither can He act there and do in it what He pleases, unless it be left vacant to Him...that many do not advance in the Christian progress, because they stick at penances and particular exercises, while they neglect the love of God, which is the end.

Brother Lawrence (1641-1691)
The Practice of the Presence of God

Judas, dost thou betray me with a kiss?
Canst thou find hell about my lips? And miss
of life, just at the gates of life and bliss?

Was ever grief like mine?

George Herbert (1593-1633)
From The Sacrifice
The Poems of George Herbert

Jesus did not need to say more than 'There am I' to make His disciples come together. They liked to be where He was. How the presence of the Mother sitting by adds to the children's joy at their play! So it is with Christ and His disciples. 'In the midst.' He is the very soul and heart of the meeting. In the worship above, the Lamb is in the midst of the throne.

Andrew Bonar (1810-1892)
Heavenly Springs

Ye shall find it your only happiness, under whatever thing disturbeth and crosseth the peace of your mind, in this life to love nothing for itself, but only God for Himself. It is the crooked love of some harlots, that they love bracelets, earrings, and rings better than the love that sendeth them. God will not so be loved; for that were to behave as harlots, and not as the chaste spouse, to abate from our love when these things are pulled away. Our love to Him should begin on earth, as it shall be in heaven; for the bride taketh not, by a thousand degrees, so much delight in her wedding garment, as she doth in her bridegroom.

Samuel Rutherford (1600-1661)
Letter XXI

The presence of God can be reached rather by the heart and by love than by understanding – In the way of God, thoughts count for little, love is everything.

Brother Lawrence (1614-1691)
The Practice of the Presence of God

Nothing is of value in His sight unless it comes out of a heart of love.

Dr. Martyn Lloyd-Jones (1900-1981)
The Unsearchable Riches of Christ

They are darkened in their understanding and separated from the life of God because of the ignorance that is in them due to the hardening of their hearts. In a word – goodness is only a sound, and virtue a mere strife of natural passions – till the Spirit of Love is the breath of everything that lives and moves in the heart. For Love is the one only blessing and goodness, and God of nature – and you have no true religion, are no worshipper of the one true God – but *in* and *by* that Spirit of Love – which is God Himself living and working *in* you.

William Law (1686-1761)
The Spirit of Love

For in Christ Jesus, neither circumcision nor uncircumcision has any value. The only thing that counts is faith expressing itself through love.

Galatians 5:6 NIV

This Holy Spark of the Divine Nature within him has a natural, strong and almost infinite tendency, or reaching after that eternal Light and Spirit of God from whence it came forth. It came forth from God, it came out of God, it partaketh of the divine nature, and therefore it is always in a state of tendency and return to God. And all this is called the breathing, the moving, the quickening of the Holy Spirit within us, which are so many operations of this Spark of Life tending towards God.

William Law (1686-1761)
The Spirit of Prayer

And this is what our Lord showed in the completeness of the love in which He holds us, that He loves us as much now while we are here as He will do when we are there in His blessed Presence. Failure of love on our part is the only cause of our suffering.

Julian of Norwich (1342-1416)
Revelations of Divine Love

There is nothing more simple, safe, pleasant and influential than this life of the heart – which is not the result of reading, or mental exertion, but is thoroughly known and experienced by dying to the creature, and love to the Creator – It is consequently more the work of the Spirit of Jesus *in* us, than our own work.

Gerhard Tersteegen (1697-1769)
Life and Character

Chapter 9

Scripture

*The most, says Martin Boos, read their Bibles
like cows that stand in the thick grass, and
trample under their feet the finest flowers
and herbs.*

Psalm 119
The Treasury of David

The essence of the authority of scripture is its ability to compel us to believe and to obey it.

Wayne Grudem (1948-)
Systematic Theology

'This is My beloved Son, hear Him'

It was worthwhile opening heaven to utter these words.

Andrew Bonar (1810-1892)
Heavenly Springs
12th Sunday

Bind them upon your heart forever;
fasten them around your neck.
When you walk, they will guide you:
when you sleep, they will watch over you;
when you awake, they will speak to you;
for these commands are a lamp,
this teaching is a light
and the corrections of discipline
are the way to life.

Proverbs 6:21 NIV

Our ultimate conviction that the words of the Bible are God's words comes only when the Holy Spirit speaks in and through the words of the Bible to our hearts and gives us an inner assurance that these are the words of our Creator speaking to us. Can you say that when you read your Bible you hear the voice of your Creator speaking to you in a way that is true of no other book?

Wayne Grudem (1948-)
Systematic Theology

How does it appear that the Scriptures have a Divine authority stamped upon them?

Its antiquity;
Its miraculous preservation in all ages;
The mystery of scripture is so obtuse and profound that no angel or man would have known it;
Its predictions which were fulfilled;
The impartiality of the men who wrote it – telling of that which reflects dishonor on themselves;
The mighty power and efficacy that the Word has had upon souls and consciences of men. It has changed their hearts;
The miracles by which Scripture is confirmed.

Thomas Watson (1620-1686)
A Body of Divinity

Christian faith has appeared to many an easy thing; nay, not a few even reckon it among the social virtues, as it were; and this they do because they have not made proof of it experimentally, and have never tasted of what efficacy (power, effectiveness) it is. For it is not possible for any man to write well about it, or to understand well what is rightly written, who has not at some time tasted of its spirit, under the pressure of tribulation: while he who has tasted of it, even to a very small extent, can never write, speak, think, or hear about it sufficiently. For it is a living fountain, springing up unto eternal life, as Christ calls it in John 4.

Martin Luther (1483-1546)

The Scripture is to be its own interpreter, or rather the Spirit speaking in it. Nothing can cut the diamond but the diamond; nothing can interpret Scripture but Scripture.

Thomas Watson (1620-1686)
A Body of Divinity

*There are some verses that are like boxes of jewels –
five great words* – Joshua 22:5 KJV

Love   Walk   Keep   Cleave   Serve

Amy Carmichael (1867-1951)
Whispers of His Power

The mystery of Scripture is so abstruse (difficult to
understand, obscure) and profound that no man or
angel would have known it, had it not been divinely
revealed. That eternity should be born, that He who
thunders in the heavens should cry in the cradle; that
He who rules the stars should suck the breasts; that
the Prince of Life should die; that the Lord of Glory
should be put to shame; that sin should be punished
to the full, yet pardoned to the full; who could ever
have conceived of such a mystery, had not the
Scripture revealed it to us?

Thomas Watson (1620-1686)
A Body of Divinity

Welcome, all Wonders in one sight!
    Eternity shut in a span.
Summer in Winter, Day in Night,
    Heaven in earth, and God in Man.
Great little one! whose all-embracing birth
    Lifts earth to heaven, stoops heav'n to earth.

Richard Crashaw (1612-1649)
from Carmen de Nostro

Why was the Son of God made man? – It was because Man was to be made again a Divine Creature. Why did Man want such a Savior? – It was because he was become earthly, mortal, gross flesh and blood. Now take Christ in this light, and consider Man in this state – and then all that is said in the Gospel stands in the fullest light.

William Law (1686-1761)
The Way to Divine Knowledge

Thus, my friend, you see the importance of this one point – Moses and the prophets have no ground or reason but this: that man had lost his Divine life and this same Divine life is to be born again in him. Now seeing this is the ground and reason of Scriptures, therefore it is the unerring key to the right use of them. They have only this one intent – to make man know, resist, and abhor the working of his fallen, earthly nature – and to turn the faith, hope and longing desire of his heart to God;

And therefore, we are only to read them with this view and to learn this one lesson from them.

William Law (1686-1761)
The Way to Divine Knowledge

'Come unto Me, all you that labour, and are weary and heavy laden, and I will refresh you." I will bring to Life that first happy state which you have lost. This is the note, the Paraphrase, the Expositor, the key to the true sense of every doctrine of Christ; which, though variously expressed to awaken the Heart, is only one and the same thing.

William Law (1686-1761)
The Way to Divine Knowledge

If your knowledge of the Scriptures and of the doctrines of the gospel of the Lord Jesus Christ has not brought you to this knowledge of the love of Christ, you should be profoundly dissatisfied and disturbed. All biblical doctrine is about this blessed Person; and there is not a greater snare in the Christian life than to forget the Person Himself and to live simply on truths concerning Him.

Martyn Lloyd-Jones (1900-1981)
The Unsearchable Riches of Christ

Learning will not beguile Christ. The Bible beguiled the Pharisees, and so may I be misled.

Samuel Rutherford (1600-1661)
Letter CVI to Lady Kenmure

The Beautitudes

They are an advanced doctorate in Christianity. They describe the mind and heart of Christ. Until we put to death our old man and until we have the real Spirit of Christ Himself living in us – we are incapable of obeying them.

Unknown

...but the Christian, who knows that the real poverty of man consists in his having lost the riches and greatness of his first life, knows that to this poor man the gospel is preached, because he only, who is sensible of this poverty, can hear and receive it. For to the man – insensible of his fallen state – the Glad Tidings of the Gospel are but like news from Fairyland, and the cross of Christ can only be a stumbling block and foolishness to him whether he be a Christian, a Jew, or a Greek.

William Law (1686-1761)
The Way to Divine Knowledge

The Bible makes more of the death of Jesus than of His life and His teaching – because the teaching of Jesus does not apply to you and me unless we have received His Spirit. What is the good of telling me to love my enemies? I hate them! To be fathomless pure in heart? To have no unworthy motive? The teaching of Jesus is for the Life He puts in, and I receive that Life by means of the cross.

Oswald Chambers (1874-1917)
Conformed to His Image

No matter how clever and well educated a man is – as long as he is not regenerated, this book is a mystery to him...On the day he receives the Lord, he can begin to understand the Bible.

...only one part within our whole being can study the Bible - our regenerated spirit.

Watchman Nee (1903-1972)
How to Study the Bible Chapter 1

It is the Spirit, who gives life; the flesh profits nothing; the words which I have spoken to you are Spirit and are life..

John 6:63 NKV

We should never consider it a small thing to find ourselves having difficulty understanding the Bible. If we have difficulty understanding the Bible, it can only mean one thing. We are living in darkness! It is a very serious thing to read God's word and not understand or receive any light from it.

Watchman Nee (1903-1972)
How to Study the Bible

The light shines in the darkness, but the darkness has not understood it.

John 1:5 NIV

Whenever a man misses two or three opportunities to obey God, he suffers loss before God...God is never short of light, but whenever He sees any unwillingness in our part...the Holy Spirit will shy away; He will retreat and not release Himself in a cheap way.

Watchman Nee (1903-1972)

What is consecration? It is serving Jehovah alone. A man cannot serve two masters...whatever we hold on to most dearly should go first.

If a man is not consecrated, he can never read the Bible well. As soon as he opens the Bible, he will come across places that he has held back in consecration, and darkness will be with him...A man does not know because he does not want to take God's way.

...The more we obey Him, the more light we will receive.

Watchman Nee (1903-1972)
How to Study the Bible

Obedience to God's word always marks a genuine believer.

John MacArthur

All grace grows as love to the word of God grows.

Phillip Henry
Father of Matthew Henry

In the beginning was the Word, and the Word was with God, and the word was God.

John 1:1 NIV

Sometimes the simplest words of our Lord (which imply so much more than they say) suddenly take on a new power, for His words, as Deissmann says, are not separate pearls on a string of pearls, but each is a separate flash from a diamond. "Behind every word there stands for a moment Jesus Himself."

Amy Carmichael (1867-1951)
Toward Jerusalem - Notes

But the immediate Word of God has neither tone nor articulation. It is mute, silent, and unutterable. It is Jesus Christ Himself, the real and essential Word, who, in the center of the soul that is disposed for receiving Him, never for one moment ceases from His living, fruitful and divine operation.

Madame Guyon (1648-1717)
The Autobiography

When the soul is sweetly and silently employed on the truths we have read – not in reasoning, but in feeding thereon and animating the will by affection rather than fatiguing the understanding by study – when, I say, the affections are in this state – we must allow them sweetly to repose and, as it were, swallow what they have tasted. This method is, indeed, highly necessary and will advance the soul farther in a short time, than any other in a course of years.

Madame Guyon (1648-1717)
A Short Method of Prayer

Meditation chews the cud, and gets the sweetness and nutritive virtue of the word into the heart and life; This is the way the godly bring forth much fruit.

Barthomew Ashwood's Heavenly Trade

The method of reading in this state is to cease when you feel yourself recollected and remain in stillness reading but little, and always desisting when thus internally attracted.

Madame Guyon (1648-1717)

Bible Study

...whatever truth you have chosen, read only a small portion of it, endeavoring to taste and digest it – to extract the essence and substance of it and proceed no farther while any savor or relish remains in the passage. Then take up your book again and proceed as before, seldom reading more than half a page at a time. It is not the quantity that is read but the manner of reading that yields us profit. ...those who read fast, reap no more advantage than a bee would, by only skimming over the surface of the flower – instead of waiting to penetrate into it and extract its sweets. Much reading is rather for scholastic subjects than divine truths.

Madame Guyon (1648-1717)
Experiencing the Depths of Jesus Christ

Whenever the Spirit of God makes a word live to you, take time to let that word sink deep into your heart. This way is open to all.

Amy Carmichael (1867-1951)
Thou Givest – They Gather

"Lazarus, Come Forth"

We need not fear to address gospel precepts to dead sinners, since by them the Spirit gives them life.

C.H. Spurgeon (1834-1892)

I will not forget Thy precepts: for with them Thou hast quickened me.

Psalm 119:93 KJV

⁂

The ministry of the Word is the pipe or organ; the Spirit of God blowing in it, effectually changes men's heart. While Peter spoke, the Holy Ghost fell on them that heard the Word of God. (Acts 10:44) Ministers knock at the door of men's hearts, the Spirit comes with a key and opens the door. *'A certain woman named Lydia, whose heart the Lord had opened."* (Acts 16:14)

Thomas Watson (1620-1686)
A Body of Divinity

Other masters cut out work for their servants – but do not help them in their work; but our Master in Heaven doth not only give us work, but strength. God bids us serve Him and He will enable us to serve Him.

"I will put my Spirit within you and will cause you to walk in My statutes...." (Ezekiel 36:27)

The Lord doth not only fit work for us - but fits us for our work - with His command He gives power.

Thomas Watson (1620-1686)
A Body of Divinity

When – in the Word – the Spirit quickens and raises the affection...When the Spirit transforms the heart, leaving an impression of holiness upon it....When the Spirit revives the heart with comfort...the heart being warmed and inflamed in a duty is God's answering by fire.

Thomas Watson (1620-1686)
A Body of Divinity

I will delight myself in Thy statues:
I will not forget Thy word.

Psalm 119:16 KJV

"forget" I never heard of a covetous old man, who had forgotten where he had buried his treasure.

Cicero de Senectute
The Treasury of David

God's word is the glass which discovereth all spiritual deformity, and also the water and soap which washeth and scoureth it away.

Paul Bayne
The Treasury of David

The words "fear not" occur many times in the Bible. The word of God has no suggestions; only commandments.

Corrie ten Boom (1892-1983)
Don't Wrestle Just Nestle

Let us therefore hold it for certain and firmly established that the soul can do without everything except the word of God, without which none of all its wants are provided for. But having the word, it is rich and wants for nothing, since that is the word of life, of truth, of light, of peace, of justification, of salvation, of joy, of liberty, of wisdom, of virtue, of grace, of glory, and of every good thing.

Martin Luther (1483-1546)
Great Voices of The Reformation

The 23rd Psalm

...though it is but a moment's opening of the soul there are emitted truths of peace and consolation that will never be absent from the world. The twenty third Psalm is the nightingale of the Psalms. It is small, of a homely feather, singing shyly out of obscurity; but oh! It has filled the whole world with melodious joy, greater than the heart can conceive...It has charmed more griefs to rest than all the philosophy of the world. It has poured balm and consolation into the heart of the sick, of captives in dungeons, of widows in their pinching griefs, of orphans in their loneliness. Dying soldiers have died easier as it was read to them...

Henry Ward Beecher (1813-1887)
The Treasury of David

There is divinity in Scripture. It contains the marrow and quintessence of religion. It is a rock of diamonds, a mystery of piety. The lips of Scripture have grace poured into them. The Scripture speaks of faith, self-denial, and all the graces which, as a chain of pearls, adorns a Christian. It excites to holiness; it treats of another world, it gives the prospect of eternity! Oh, then, search the Scripture! Make the Word familiar to you. Had I the tongue of angels, I could not sufficiently set forth the excellency of Scripture. It is the spiritual optic-glass, in which we behold God's glory; it is the tree of life, the oracle of wisdom, the rule of manners, the heavenly seed of which the new creature is formed. "The two Testaments," says Austin, "are the two breasts which every Christian must suck, that he may get spiritual nourishment." The leaves of the tree of life were for healing. So these holy leaves of Scripture are for the healing of our souls. The Scripture is profitable for all things. If we are deserted, here is spiced wine that cheers the heavy heart; if we are pursued by Satan, here's the sword of the Spirit to resist him; if we are diseased with sin's leprosy, here are the waters of the sanctuary, both to cleanse and to cure. Oh, then, search the Scriptures!

...Read with seriousness. It is a matter of life and death; by this Word you must be tried; conscience and Scripture are the jury God will proceed by, in judging you.

Thomas Watson (1620-1686)
A Body of Divinity

In your temptations, run to the promises; they may be our Lord's branches hanging over the water, that our Lord's silly half-drowned children may take a grip of them. And those boughs never break.

Samuel Rutherford (1600-1661)
Letters

...there lie my books – for all I sought
My heart possesses now,
The words are sweet that tell Thy love,
The Love itself art Thou.

One line I read – and then no more –
I close the book to see
No more the symbol and the sign,
But Christ revealed to me

Gerhard Tersteegen (1697-1769)
from The Sabbath Year

Meditate

...but I cannot worthily and fully set forth the gracious meaning and force of this word; for this 'meditating' consists first in an intent observing of the words of the law – and then in comparing of the different scriptures – which is a certain delightful hunting, nay, rather a playing with stags in a forest – where the Lord furnishes us with the stags, and opens to us their secret coverts. And from this kind of employment, there comes forth at length, a man well instructed in the law of the Lord, to speak to the people.

Martin Luther (1483-1546)
Psalm 1:2
Treasury of David

God's word will stand, and we shall get nothing by disputing it, or delaying to submit to it.

Matthew Henry (1662-1714)

Psalm 1 NIV

"Blessed is the man who does not walk in the counsel of the wicked or stand in the way of sinners or sit in the seat of mockers. But his delight is in the law of the Lord, and on His law he meditates day and night..."

The psalmist says more to the point about true happiness in this short Psalm than any one of the philosophers, or all of them put together; for they did but beat the bush, God has here put the bird into our hand.

John Trapp

Chapter 10

Humility

That Christ Who would not endure sin in the angels, should Himself endure to have sin imputed to Him is the most amazing humility that ever was.

Thomas Watson
A Body of Divinity

from Holy Sonnet XV

'Twas much, that man was made
    like God before
But that God should be made
    like man, much more.

John Donne (1572-1631)

Christ never rode in triumph into Jerusalem, but when he came thither to suffer, nor had His head anointed, but for His burial.

Matthew Henry's
Commentary Mark 14:1-3

As a prisoner for the Lord, then, I urge you to live a life worthy of the calling you have received. Be completely humble and gentle; be patient, bearing with one another in love.

Ephesians 4:2 NIV

For so the proud man saith, I will be like the highest (Isaiah 14) and, if he could, above the highest too. This is the creature that was taken out of the dust (Genesis 2:7) and so soon as he was made, he opposed himself against that majesty which the angels adore, the thrones worship, the devils fear, and the heavens obey. How many sins are in this sinful world! and yet, as Solomon saith of the good wife (Proverbs 31:29) *"many daughters have done virtuously, but thou, surmountest them all;"* so may I say of pride...many sins have done wickedly, but thou surmounted them all; for the wrathful man, the prodigal man, the lascivious man, the surfeiting man, the slothful man, is rather an enemy to himself than God, but the proud man sets himself against God, because He doth against His laws; He maketh himself equal with God, because he doth all without God, and craves no help of Him; he exalteth himself above God, because he will have his own will though it be contrary to God's will.

Henry Smith (1560-1591)
The Treasury of David

The highest glory of the creature is in being only a vessel to receive and enjoy and show forth the glory of God. It can do this only as it is willing to be nothing in itself, that God may be all.....If you would enter into full fellowship with Christ in His death, and know the full deliverance from self – humble yourself. Place yourself before God in your utter helplessness – consent heartily to the fact of your impotence to slay or make alive yourself – sink down into your own nothingness in the spirit of meek and patient, trustful surrender to God...for nothing is in vain or without profit to the humble soul; it stands always in a state of divine growth – everything that falls upon it is like a dew of heaven to it...Accept every humiliation, look upon every fellow man who tries or vexes you, as a means of grace to humble you. Use every opportunity of humbling yourself before your fellow man as a help to abide humble before God.

Andrew Murray (1828-1917)
Humility

Since the first day that you set your mind to gain understanding and to humble yourself before your God, your words were heard.

Daniel 10:12 NIV

So much as you have of pride within you, you have of the fallen angel alive in you; so much as you have of true humility, so much you have of the Lamb of God within you.

William Law (1687-1761)

We shall see that we may indeed have strong intellectual conviction and assurance of the truth, while pride is kept in the heart, but that it makes the living faith, which has power with God, an impossibility.

Andrew Murray (1828-1917)
Humility

We are too high; Lord Jesus, we implore Thee,
  Make of us something like the low green moss,
That vaunted not, a quiet thing before Thee,
  Cool for Thy feet sore wounded at the Cross.

Amy Carmichael (1867-1951)
Toward Jerusalem

The truly humble soul is not surprised at its defects or failings, and the more miserable it beholds itself, the more it abandons itself to God and presses for a more intimate alliance with Him, seeing the need it has of His aid. It is of great importance to guard against vexation on account of our faults; it springs from a secret root of pride and a love of our own excellence; we are hurt at feeling what we are.

Madame Guyon (1648-1717)
Experiencing the Depths of Jesus Christ

The Task
Philippians 3:7

To learn and yet to learn, whilst life goes by.
So pass the student's days;
And thus be great, and do great things and die,
And be embalmed with praise.

My work is but to lose and to forget,
Thus small, despised to be;
All to unlearn – this task before me set;
Unlearn all else but Thee.

Gerhard Tersteegen (1697-1769)
Hymns of Tersteegen and Others

Chapter 11

Sanctification

Blessed are the undefiled in the way, who walk in the law of the Lord.

Psalm 119:1 KJV

"the undefiled". You ask, Why does God will that we be undefiled? I reply, because He has chosen us for Himself, for servants, for spouses, for temples.

Thomas LeBlanc
The Treasury of David
Psalm 119:1 KJV

It is the great design God carries on in the world to make a people like Himself in holiness. What are the showers of ordinances for, but to rain down righteousness upon us, and make us holy. What are the promises for, but to encourage holiness? What is the sending of the Spirit into the world for, but to anoint us with holy unction (1 John 2:20). What are all affliction for, but to make us partake of God's holiness? (Hebrews 12:10) What are the mercies for but loadstones to draw us to holiness? What is the end of Christ's dying, but that His blood might wash away our unholiness. Who gave Himself for us, to purify unto Himself a peculiar people. (Titus 2:14) So that if we are not holy, we cross God's great design in the world.

Thomas Watson (1620-1686)
A Body of Divinity

Indeed, the more sanctified the person is, the more conformed he is to the image of His Savior, the more he must recoil against every lack of conformity to the holiness of God. The deeper his apprehension of the majesty of God, the greater the intensity of his love to God, the more persistent his yearning for the attainment of the prize of the high calling of God in Christ Jesus, the more conscious will he be of the gravity of the sin that remains and the more poignant will be his detestation of it...Was this not the effect in all the people of God as they came into closer proximity to the revelation of God's holiness? In practical terms, this means that we must affirm two things to be true. On the one hand, we will never be able to say, "I am completely free from sin," because our sanctification will never be completed. But on the other hand a Christian should never say (for example), "This sin has defeated me. I give up. I have had a bad temper for thirty seven years, and I will have one until the day I die, and people are just going to have to put up with me the way I am!" To say this is to say that sin has gained dominion. It is to allow sin to reign in our bodies. It is to admit defeat. It is to deny the truth of Scripture, which tell us, "*You also must consider yourselves dead to sin and alive to God in Christ Jesus*" (Romans 6:11) – that "*sin will have no dominion over you.*" (Romans 6:14)

Wayne Grudem (1948 -)
Systematic Theology

The greater an individual's comparative holiness, the more intense will be his longing for absolute holiness.

Hugh Moffat
The Treasury of David
Psalm 119:32

Let us also, at the same time, pray – and that more with the heart than the mouth; especially for the Spirit of Jesus, that He may rule and work in us. It is He who alone can lead us into all truth, and will do so; without Him, it would be impossible for us to continue, or perform anything good.

Gerhard Tersteegen (1697-1769)
Letters and Writings

So do not fear for I am with you;
Do not be dismayed for I am your God.
I will strengthen you and help you .
I will uphold you with My righteous right hand.

Isaiah 41:10 NIV

God's Requirements
Deuteronomy 10-11 NIV

And now O Israel, what does the Lord your God
ask of you:

Fear the Lord your God;
Love Him and keep His requirements always;
Walk in all His ways;
Serve the Lord your God with all your heart and
with all your soul;
Observe the Lord's commands and decrees;
Circumcise your hearts;
Do not be stiffnecked any longer;
Love those who are aliens;
Hold fast to Him;
Rejoice before the Lord your God in everything
you put your hand to.

Confusion arises when we disassociate ourselves
from our Lord, and try to live up to a standard merely
constructed on His word.

Oswald Chambers (1874-1917)
The Complete Works of Oswald Chambers

I am the Lord who makes you holy.

Leviticius 20:8 NIV

Commit your way to the Lord; trust in Him and <u>He</u> will do this: He will make your righteousness shine like the dawn...

Psalm 37:5 NIV

The hardest things in the world are not too hard for the Lord. God never made a creature but that when it is marred, He can make it all over again. He created all men, and when they are dissolved into dust, He can restore them to the very same life and the same bodies He created. Nature is His own proper handiwork, and when nature halts and crooks* in its going, He can heal and make it go straight. Christ is as good at the second as at the first creation.

Samuel Rutherford (1600-1661)
The Power of Faith and Prayer

*is crippled and turns out of the straight course

...that Jesus Christ died to deliver us from this present evil world (Galatians 1:4). We are apt to think Christ died to deliver us only from hell, and if that be done, we are well enough. No – Christ died to deliver us from *this world.* So if our hearts are glued to present things, and our affections fixed upon them, we do directly thwart the great design of our Lord Jesus Christ in coming to save us.

From a letter by Matthew Henry
To a friend – forward – Vol. 1, p. 21
Matthew Henry's Commentary

For if goodness can only be *in* God – if it cannot exist separate from Him – if He can only bless and sanctify – not by a creaturely gift – but by <u>Himself</u> becoming the blessing and sanctification of the creature, - then it is the highest degree of blindness, to look for any goodness or happiness from anything but the immediate indwelling, union, and operation of the Diety *in* the life of the creature.

William Law (1686-1761)
The Spirit of Love

Christ <u>in</u> you, the hope of glory.

Colossians 1:27 NIV

...self-denials and mortifications – as to their nature and considered <u>in themselves</u>, they have nothing of Goodness or Holiness – nor are they any real parts of our sanctification- they are not the true food or nourishment of the divine life in our souls. They have no Quickening, Sanctifying power in them. Their only worth consists in this – that they remove the <u>impediments</u> of Holiness, break down that which stands between God and us, and make way for the quickening , sanctifying Spirit of God to operate on our souls - which operation of God is the one <u>only</u> thing that can raise the Divine Life in the soul, or help it to the smallest degree of real holiness or spiritual life.

William Law (1686- 1761)
The Spirit of Prayer

For It Is God Who Works in You

Philippians 2:13 NIV

Although the believer is responsible to work, the Lord actually produces good works and spiritual fruit in the lives of believers. (John 15:5, 1 Corinthians 12:6) This is accomplished because He works through us by His *in*dwelling Spirit (Acts 1:8, 1 Corinthians 3:16, 17; 6:19, 20, Colossians 3:13) *to will and to do.* God energizes both the believer's desires and his action.

John MacArthur
The MacArthur Study Bible NKJ

Commit your way to the Lord; trust in Him and He will do this: He will make your righteousness shine like the dawn.

Psalm 37:5 NIV

Your business is now to give way to this heavenly working of the Spirit of God in your soul, and turn from everything – either within you, or without you – that may hinder the further awakening of all that is holy and heavenly within you.

William Law (1686-1761)
The Way to Divine Knowledge

Ah, what anxiety do many exemplify, and what pains they take to become holy by their own efforts! O my dear friends – all you have to do is to love Christ and unite yourself with Him, by faith, love, and prayer, as the branch is united to the vine. ...we have only to love Him to remain inwardly secluded in His love, and as barren branches in ourselves, let the pure and divine influence and power of the precious love of Christ, penetrate our whole souls. We should then become, as though naturally, a people dear and acceptable to God, and filled with all the precious fruit of righteousness, to the praise of Jesus Christ...and really, if it were possible, that we could become holy by our own efforts, yet all would be an imperfect, morbid, and worthless phantom, proceeding from the will and power of man, in which we only regarded and loved ourselves. It is the love of Christ which must impart true life, power and value to all our godliness, works and virtues.

Gerhard Tersteegen (1697-1769)
Life and Writings

All this, because this simple tendency or inward inclination of your heart to sink down into patience, meekness, humility and resignation to God, is truly giving up all that you are and all that you have from fallen Adam, to follow and be with Christ; it is your highest act of faith in Him, and love to Him, the most ardent and earnest declaration of your cleaving to Him with all your heart, and seeking no salvation but in Him and from Him. And therefore, all the good and blessing, pardon and deliverance from sin, that ever happened to anyone, from any kind or degree of faith and hope, and application of Christ – is sure to be had from this state of heart - which stands continually turned to Him, in a hunger and desire of being led and governed by His Spirit of patience, meekness, humility and resignation to God.

William Law (1686-1761)
The Spirit of Love

When we will run most, even spiritually, we do not bring home richest mercies. Early rising, night watching, even in this spiritual laboring, often has not the richest reward – because God will have free-will's natural sweating cried down and grace to shine like heaven – and because we are ready to sacrifice to *ourselves* and not to burn incense to Christ and His free grace.

Samuel Rutherford (1600-1661)
The Power of Faith and Prayer

Our Lord said, "I am the Way" – not the way to anyone or anything. He is not a way we leave behind us. He is the Way to the Father *in* which we abide. (John 15:4) He *is* the Way, not He *was* the Way – and there is not any way of living *in the* Fatherhood of God, except by living *in Him.*

Unknown

...continue to live in Him – rooted and built up in Him.

Colossians 2:6 NIV

With Him, All Things

Hath not each heart, a passion and a dream?
        Each some companionship for ever sweet?
And each in saddest skies some silver gleam,
        And each some passing joy, too fair and fleet?
And each a staff and stay, though frail it prove,
        And each a face he fain would ever see?
And what have I? An endless Heaven of love,
        A rapture, and a glory, and a calm;
A life that is an everlasting Psalm,
        All O Beloved, in Thee.

Gerhard Tersteegen (1697-1769)
Hymns of Tersteegen and Others

Since entering upon the religious life, I no longer
perplex myself with thoughts of virtue, or of my
salvation. But having given myself wholly to God, to
make what satisfaction I could for my sins, and for love
of Him – having renounced all that is not His, I have
come to see that my only business is to live as though
there were none but He and I in the world.

Brother Lawrence (1614-1691)
The Practice of the Presence of God

Some Christians overlook the blessings of sanctification and yet to a thoroughly renewed heart, this is one of the sweetest gifts of the covenant. If we could be saved from wrath and yet remain unregenerate, unrepentant sinners, we should not be saved as we desire, for we mainly and chiefly pant to be saved from sin and led in the way of holiness.

C.H. Spurgeon (1834-1892)
The Treasury of David
Psalm 23:3

Blessed are the pure in heart; for they shall see God.

Matthew 5:8 KJV

Purity of heart is heaven begun in a man.

Thomas Watson (1620-1686)
The Beatitudes

For Christ possessed by faith here is young heaven and glory in the bud.

Samuel Rutherford (1600-1661)

...from the manner in which some men unguardedly preach the covenant, we might infer that God would bless a certain set of men – however, they might live, and however, they might neglect His law – But the word teaches not so. The covenant is not legal, but it is holy. It is all of grace from first to last, yet it is no panderer to sin; on the contrary, one of its greatest promises is, "I will put my laws in their hearts, and in their minds will I write them." Its general aim is the sanctifying of a people unto God, zealous for good works, and all its gifts and operations work in that direction. Faith keeps the covenant by looking alone to Jesus, while at the same time by earnest obedience it remembers the Lord's commandments to do them.

C.H. Spurgeon (1834-1892)
The Treasury of David

Holiness of character, chastity of life, living communion with God – that is the end of a man's life – whether he is happy or not is a matter of moonshine.

Oswald Chambers (1874-1917)
Complete Works

You are never more like God then when you forgive.

Unknown

We have faith in Jesus to save us – but do we prove that He has saved us by living a new life? I say that I believe that Jesus can do this and that; well has He done it? Are *we* monuments to the grace of God, or do we only experience God's supernatural power in our work for Him.

Oswald Chambers (1874-1917)
Conformed to His Image

Men do not become holy by a careless wish: there must be study, consideration, deliberation, and earnest enquiry, or the way of truth will be missed.

C.H. Spurgeon (1834-1892)
The Treasury of David

Being confident of this very thing, that He which hath begun a good work in you will perform it until the day of Jesus Christ.

Philippians 1:6 KJV

Is not this a perfect word? Bishop Moule says the Greek word translated "will perform it" means "will evermore put His finishing touches to it." Think of the fingers that made the blue of the kingfisher's wings, and every other lovely thing on earth, putting finishing touches to you and to me today. Is there one of us who would hinder him?

These finishing touches often come through the sweet joys of life, but they come, too, through the tiny trials, the little disappointments, the small things we hardly like to speak about, and yet which are very real to us. Let us think of them as the touches of his fingers – the finishing touches.

Amy Carmichael (1867-1951)
Edges of His Ways

Chapter 12

The Fear of the Lord

He who fears God has nothing else to fear.

C.H. Spurgeon

The fear of the Lord is the beginning of knowledge; but fools despise wisdom and instruction.

Proverbs 1:7 KJV

It is its first principle, but it is also its head and chief attainment....to know God so as to walk aright before Him is the greatest of all the applied sciences.

C.H. Spurgeon (1834-1892)

Wisdom is like God's daughter, that He giveth to the man who loveth her, and sueth * for her and meaneth to set her at his heart.

Henry Smith

* as a suitor, a wooer

Those eyes which have no fear of God before them now, shall have the terrors of hell before them forever.

C.H Spurgeon (1834-1892)
Psalm 36:1
The Treasury of David

The fear of the Lord tendeth to Life.

Proverbs 19:23 KJV

If the fear of the Lord (the reverence of the Lord) tends to life, then anything irreverent tends to death. It is to death that the devil is continually seeking to lure us.

Amy Carmichael (1867-1951)
Whispers of His Power

Serve the Lord with fear and rejoice with trembling.

Psalm 2:11 KJV

There must ever be a holy fear mixed with the Christian's joy. This is a sacred compound yielding a sweet smell, and we must see to it that we burn no other upon the altar. Fear, without joy, is torment: and joy without holy fear would be presumption.

C.H. Spurgeon (1834-1892)
The Treasury of David

The secret of the Lord is with them that fear Him and He shall show them His covenant.

Psalm 25:14 KJV

And what is this secret? It is that in God, which the world neither knows nor sees, nor cares to enjoy. It is His mind revealed to those that love Him, His plans, His ways, and thoughts opened to them.

Mary B.M. Duncan

The Lord confides in those who fear Him. He makes His covenant known to them.

Psalm 25:14 KJV

Many profess godliness, but are little the better for it, because they have not the true secret of it: he hath that, with whom God is in secret in his heart: and he that is righteous in secret, where no man sees him, he is the righteous man with whom *the secret of the Lord is.*

Michael Jermine (1591-1659)
The Treasury of David

As a father has compassion on his children, so the Lord has compassion on those who fear Him.

Psalm 103:13 NIV

We do not adore a God of stone, but the living God, who is tenderness itself.

C.H. Spurgeon (1834-1892)
The Treasury of David

Fear means "reverenced" it means the deep awe, which love so tender, yet so holy, must needs inspire. It means that kind of love which has fear and reverence in it, and that kind of love will never think it is little thing to grieve our holy God.

If we have been defeated, let us not be discouraged, there is forgiveness. But do not think lightly of defeat, as though it did not much matter. It cost God Calvary to forgive my "smallest sin."

Amy Carmichael (1867-1951)
Edges of His Ways

It is neither learning nor labour that can give insight into God's secrets. These things come by revelation rather than by discourse of reason, and must therefore be obtained by prayer. Those that diligently seek Him shall be of His Cabinet Council, shall know His soul secrets, and be admitted into a gracious familiarity and friendship.

John Trapp
The Treasury of David

He who hath received from the Lord grace to fear Him may be bold to seek any necessary good thing from Him; because the fear of God hath annexed the promises of all other blessings with it.

William Cowper
The Treasury of David

But this is the man to whom I will look and have regard: he who is humble and of a broken or wounded spirit, and who trembles at My word and reveres my command.

Isaiah 66:2 Amplified

Many think they believe, but never tremble; the devils are farther on than these. (James 2:19)

Samuel Rutherford (1600-1661)
Letter CLXXX

Chapter 13

The Manifest Presence
of God

Because He hath set His love upon Me –
Because He hath known My name –

The two folding doors of the secret place
of the Most High.

Andrew Bonar
Proverbs 1:7 KJV

Are you often in Heaven? Often with Christ? Or were you all your days on this side of time with the creature?

Samuel Rutherford (1600-1661)
The Power of Faith and Prayer

If you have not two heavens, you will never have one. If you have not a heaven here you will never have one yonder.

Andrew Bonar (1810-1892)
Heavenly Springs
12th Sunday

Who has not found the heaven below
    Will fail of it above.
God's residence is next to mine,
    His furniture is love.

Emily Dickinson (1830-1886)
Collected Poems LXIX

Fellowship with the living God is a distinguishing feature in the holiness given by the Holy Ghost; we get access by one Spirit to the Father through Him.

Andrew Bonar (1810-1892)

Personal communion with God is the end of our graces; for as reason and the intercourse of it makes men sociable one with another, so the divine nature makes us sociable with God Himself; and the life we live by is but an engine, a glass to bring God down to us.

Thomas Goodwin
Psalm 63:1
The Treasury of David

He who has clean hands and a pure heart. Who does not lift up his soul to an idol or swear by what is false. He will receive blessing from the Lord and vindication from God His Savior.

Psalm 24:4,5 NIV

The pure in heart shall *see God,* all others are but blind bats; stone-blindness in the eyes arises from stone in the heart.

C.H. Spurgeon (1834-1892)
Psalm 24:4

There are the common frames and feelings of repentance, and faith and joy and hope which are enjoyed by the entire family, but there is an upper realm of rapture, of communion and conscious union with Christ, which is far from being the common dwelling-place of believers....there are heights in *experimental* knowledge of the things of God which the eagle's eye of *acumen and philosophic thought hath never seen: God alone can bear us there, but the chariot in which He takes us up and the fiery steeds with which that chariot is dragged, are prevailing prayers.

C.H. Spurgeon (1834-1892)
Morning & Evening

* acumen – an ability to judge well

The morning watch must not be regarded as an end in itself. Although it gives us a blessed time for prayer and Bible study and brings us a certain measure of refreshment and help; that is not enough. It is to serve to secure the presence of Christ for the whole day.

Andrew Muray (1828-1917)
The Inner Life

I see that I will need everyday more and more in the morning, before any business begins, a cup of the new wine of the kingdom – fellowship with God.

Andrew Bonar (1810-1892)
Heavenly Springs

It is meeting with the Lord personally, face to face, that gives rest. The blood gives the conscience rest, but the heart craves something more, and that is fellowship with Him who gave us that atoning blood and sprinkled it on our souls.

Andrew Bonar (1810-1892)
Heavenly Springs

O His perfumed face, His fair face, His lovely and kindly kisses have made me, a poor prisoner, see that there is more to be had of Christ *in this life* than I believed.

Samuel Rutherford (1600-1661)
Letters

The most holy practice, the nearest to daily life, and the most essential for the spiritual life, is the practice of the presence of God, that is, to find joy in His divine company, and to make it a habit of life, speaking humbly, and conversing lovingly with Him at all times, every moment, without rule or restriction, above all at time of temptation, distress, dryness and revulsion, and even of faithlessness and sin.

Brother Lawrence (1614-1691)
The Practice of the Presence of God

...that when we see God, we have what we desire, and then we do not need to pray.

Julian of Norwich (1342-1416)

Many of you will be having your Quiet Time as I write. May each one touch at least the border of His garment. One knows when one has done that. It is different from just reading or even just praying. Something happens when we touch. What happens? Who can tell? Only we know that something has passed from Him to us – courage to do the difficult thing we had feared to do; patience to bear with that trying one; fortitude to carry on when we felt we could not; sweetness, inward happiness, peace.

Amy Carmichael (1867-1951)
Thou Givest – They Gather

His very countenance was edifying – such a sweet and calm devotion appearing in it, as could not but affect the beholder. And it was observed that in the greatest hurry of business in the kitchen, he still preserved his recollection and heavenly-mindedness. He was never hasty nor loitering, but did each thing in its season, with an even, uninterrupted composure and tranquillity of spirit. The time of business said he, does not with me differ from the time of prayer and in the noise and clutter of my kitchen, while several persons are at the same time, calling for different things, I possess God in as great tranquillity as if I were upon my knees at the Blessed Sacrament.

Brother Lawrence (1619-1691)
The Practice of the Presence of God
Fourth Conversation

Yet furthermore, I count everything a loss compared to the possession of the priceless privilege (the overwhelming preciousness, the surpassing worth, and supreme advantage) of knowing Christ Jesus, my Lord and of progressively becoming more deeply acquainted with Him (of perceiving and recognizing and understanding Him more fully and clearly). For His sake I have lost everything, and consider it all to be mere rubbish (refuse, dregs) in order that I may win (gain) Christ the Anointed One.

Philippians 3:8 Amplified

Chapter 14

When I Am Weak

.... My grace is sufficient for you,
for My power is made perfect in weakness.

2 Corinthians 12:9 NIV

There is a great difference between the weakness of grace and the want (lack) of grace. A man may have life, though he be sick and weak. Weak grace is not to be despised, but cherished. Christ will not break the bruised reed. Do not argue from the weakness of grace to the nullity.

(1). Weak grace will give us a title to Christ as well as strong.

(2). Weak faith is capable of growth. The seed springs up by degrees, first the blade, and then the ear, and then the full corn in the ear. The faith that is strongest was once in its infancy. ...

(3). The weakest grace shall persevere as well as the strongest. A child was as safe in the ark as Noah.

An infant believer that is but newly laid to the breast of the promise, is as safe in Christ as the most eminent heroic saint.

William Law (1686-1761)
The Lord's Prayer
Second Petition

The first attempt to render spiritual obedience will, quickly convince us of our utter helplessness.

Charles Bridges
The Treasury of David
Psalm 119:5

The greatest spiritual blessing we receive is when we come to the knowledge that we are destitute.

Oswald Chambers (1874-1917)
My Utmost for His Highest – Updated Version

Hold yourself in prayer before God like a dumb or paralytic beggar at a rich man's gate.

Brother Lawrence (1614-1691)
The Practice of the Presence of God
Eighth Letter

God's love is just His delight to impart Himself and His blessedness to His children. Come, and however feeble you feel, just wait in His Presence. As a feeble, sickly invalid is brought out into the sunshine to let its warmth go through him, come with all that is dark and cold in you into the sunshine of God's holy omnipotent love.

Andrew Murray (1828-1917)
Waiting on God
Eighth Day

So do not fear for I am with you;
Do not dismayed for I am your God.
I will strengthen you and help you
I will uphold you with My righteous right hand.

Isaiah 41:10 NIV

What God hath required at our hands, that we may desire at His hands. God is no Pharaoh to require brick where He giveth no straw....The law giveth no strength to perform anything, but the gospel offereth grace.

Thomas Merton
The Treasury of David
Psalm 119:5

For thus said the Lord God, the Holy One of Israel: in returning [to Me] and resting [in Me] you shall be saved; in quietness and in [trusting] confidence shall be your strength.

Isaiah 30:15 Amplified

Live retired in the center of your hearts with God, as innocent children, who though unable to reason, yet possess much love and affection; and as such suck the breasts of divine love.

Gerhard Tersteegen (1697-1769)
Letters

The more I saw my own misery, incapacity and nothingness, the plainer it appeared that they rendered me fitter for the design of God, whatever they might be. "O my Lord," said I, "take the weak and wretched to do Thy works, that Thou mayst have all the glory and that man may attribute nothing of them to himself. If Thou shouldst take a person of eminence and great talents, one might attribute to him something – but if Thou takest me, it will manifest that Thou alone art the Author of whatever good shall be done."

I continued quiet in my spirit – leaving the whole affair to God – being satisfied, if He should require anything of me – that He would furnish me with the means of performing it.

Madame Guyon (1648-1717)
The Autobiography

Christ only makes His bride experience her own weakness, that she may lose all strength and all support in herself, and that, in her self-despair, He may carry her in His arms, and she may be willing to be thus borne, for whatever her course may be, she walks as a child - But when she is *in* God, and is borne by Him, her progress is infinite, since it is that of God Himself.

Madame Guyon (1648-1717)
Spiritual Torrents Part I

The Sun to Rule by Day

Thou sayest, "Fit me, fashion me for Thee."
Stretch forth thine empty hands and be thou still;
O restless soul, thou dost but hinder Me
By valiant purpose and by steadfast will.
Behold the summer flowers beneath the sun,
In stillness His great glory they behold;
And sweetly thus His mighty work is done,
And resting in His gladness they unfold.
So are the sweetness and the joy divine
Thine, O beloved, and *the work is Mine.*

Gerhard Tersteegen (1697-1769)
Hymns of Tersteegen and Others

As little as a child, born of human parents, is anxious how it may become great – so little ought a child of Grace to be concerned how it may grow up, and become strong and holy. The parental love of Christ provides for all this; it is only necessary that the child remain in its Mother's lap; and by prayer, faith and love, seek nourishment and strength for its life and growth – from the breasts of Divine grace. And whilst, thus lying in the lap of love, the weakest and most needy infant need not be afraid of any danger.

Gerhard Tersteegen (1697-1769)
His Letters and Writings

....So the one who feeds on Me will live because of Me.

John 6:57 NIV

At Rest

O God, a world of empty show,
        Dark wilds of restless, fruitless quest
Lie round me wheresoe'er I go;
        Within, with Thee, is rest.

And sated with the weary sum
        Of all men think, and hear, and see,
O, more than mother's heart, I come,
        A tired child to Thee.

Sweet childhood of eternal life!
        Whilst troubled days and years go by,
In stillness hushed from stir and strife,
        Within Thine Arms I lie.

Thine Arms, to whom I turn and cling
        With thirsting soul that longs for Thee;
As rain that makes the pastures sing,
        Art Thou, my God, to me

Gerhard Tersteegen (1697-1769)
Hymns of Tersteegen and Others

Wait on the Lord, be of good courage and He shall strengthen thy heart.

Psalm 27:14 KJV

Wait at His door with prayer
Wait at His foot with humility
Wait at His table with service
Wait at His window with expectancy.

C.H. Spurgeon (1834-1892)
The Treasury of David

It is safe to lean on Him, since He bears up the pillars both of heaven and earth.

C.H. Spurgeon (1834-1892)
The Treasury of David

In these pages they will not find set out a devotion which is merely speculative, or which can only be practiced in a cloister. No, there is an obligation laid on everyman to worship God and love Him, and we cannot carry out this solemn duty as we ought unless our heart is knit in love to God, and our communion is so close as to constrain us to run to Him at every moment, just like little children who cannot stand upright without their mother's arms of love.

Abbe Joseph de Beaufor
The Practice of the Presence of God

Perhaps some may wonder, "How shall I know when He is speaking to me? How can I distinguish between the voices I hear in my heart? I am not old or wise or clever, how can I know? How does a baby know the voice of the one it knows best? Is it old or wise or clever? A sheep is not a clever animal, but it knows the voice of its shepherd, and a stranger will it not follow, for it knows not the voice of strangers (John 10:4). Love is the answer to all our questions: love and we shall know.

Amy Carmichael (1867-1951)
Thou Givest – They Gather

...but you received The Spirit of sonship. And by Him we cry, "Abba, Father."

Romans 8:15 NIV

This filial (childlike) view of faith, this collectedness, and occupation of the heart with the omnipresent God of Love, and with His divine perfections, is a real stratagem in the inward conflict; by which the soul – instead of openly facing the enemy, acts as a child, that flies to its Mother at the sight of a dog, instead of fighting with it, and hides itself, with confidence, in her lap.

Gerhard Tersteegen (1697-1769)
Letters xxii

Let us also, at the same time, pray – and that more with the heart than the mouth, especially for the Spirit of Jesus, that He may rule and work in us. It is He who alone can lead us unto all truth, and will do so; without Him, it would be impossible for us to continue, or perform anything good.

Gerhard Tersteegen (1697-1769)
Life and Writings

Place no confidence whatever in your own hearts, your courage, your strength, your light, your virtues, or your faithfulness; but like myself, be as little children, who must perish, without a mother's care. All that is our own is worthless and everything else is free grace, for which we must every moment wait and partake of.

Gerhard Tersteegen (1697-1769)
Letters and Writings

....Without Me you can do nothing.

John 15:5 NIV

...My grace is sufficient for you, for My power is made perfect in weakness.

2 Corinthians 12:9 NIV

Comfort in case of weakness of grace, and fear of falling away. I pray but I cannot send out strong cries. I believe, but the hand of my faith shakes and trembles. Cannot God strengthen weak grace?

Thomas Watson (1620-1686)
A Body of Divinity

It shall be to you according as you believe, but your small, short hand and poor fingers of faith shall not be the measure. It is a little faith, but it is no little Christ that your faith lays hold on...Heaven and glory is due by promise to the child that can but creep, to Christ's sucking infants, as well as to aged men and fathers. There will be many weak citizens and many of the refuse of the flock and many tender lambs in Heaven, who may thank Christ's tender bosom that did bear them as well as strong Abraham; poor creeping Christians of England and Scotland set beside Moses, the greatest of the prophets, and David, the greatest of kingly prophets, who had a king's faith. This argues the transactions of the Gospel to be of mere grace.

Samuel Rutherford (1600-1661)
The Power of Faith and Prayer

Chapter 15

Dryness

He suffered them to hunger.

Deuteronomy 8:3

...the ebbings and flowings of God – this you may read in Solomon's Song, especially Chapter 3 and Chapter 5. There is a time when Christ is behind the wall and looks through the gates [lattice, Song 2:9] and there is a time when He comes to His garden to feast upon the honeycomb and His spiced wine, and then the spouse has a rich feast of love and of the dainties of Heaven, and is taken into the King's house and Christ's banner over her is love (Song, 2:4). "And his left hand is under 'her' head and His right hand doth embrace her (Song 2:6)...And there is a time of swooning and love – sickness and anxious questions: Watchmen, "saw ye Him whom my soul loveth?" (Song 3:3) The manifestations of God have a winter.

Samuel Rutherford (1600-1661)

That we ought to give ourselves up to God, with regard to both things temporal and spiritual, and seek our satisfaction only in the fulfilling of consolation, for all would be equal to a soul truly resigned. That there needed fidelity in those drynesses and insensibilities and the irksomeness in prayer, by which God tries our love to Him, that then was the time for us to make good and effectual acts of resignation whereof one alone would oftentimes very much promote our spiritual advancement.

Brother Lawrence (1614-1691)
The Practice of the Presence of God

Learn daily both to possess and miss Christ in His secret bridegroom – smiles. He must go and come, because His infinite wisdom thinketh it best for you. We shall be together one day.

Samuel Rutherford (1600-1661)
Letter CXCII

You must learn to swim and hold up your head above the water when the sense of His presence is not with you to hold up your chin.

Samuel Rutherford (1600-1661)
Letter CI

I would warmly recommend to all to never finish prayer without remaining some little time afterward in a respectful silence. It is also of the greatest importance for the soul to go to prayer with courage, and to bring with it such a pure and disinterested love, as seeks nothing from God, but to please Him and do His will. For a servant who only proportions his diligence to his hope of reward, is unworthy of any recompence. Go then to prayer, <u>not desiring to enjoy spiritual delights</u>, but just as it pleases God. This will preserve your tranquil spirit in <u>aridity</u>, as well as in consolation and prevent your being surprised at the apparent repulses or absence of God.

Madame Guyon (1648-1717)
Experiencing the Depths of Jesus Christ

Therefore the measures and degrees of the motions of grace are exceedingly various in one and the same soul. There will be a strong and mighty blowing of the Holy Ghost just now, and presently [immediately] after a slow, sluggish and quiet breathing, as is clear in David, who had both high feast days of entire communion with God and ordinary breathings of God as Psalm 31 and Psalm 63 compared together do make clear.

Samuel Rutherford (1600-1661)
The Power of Faith and Prayer

Jesus said there are times when God cannot lift the darkness from you, but you should trust Him. At times God will appear like an unkind friend, but He is not. He will appear like an unnatural father, but He is not; He will appear like an unjust judge, but He is not. Keep the thought that the mind of God is behind all things strong and growing. Not even the smallest detail of life happens unless God's will is behind it. Therefore you can rest in perfect confidence in Him.

Oswald Chambers (1874-1917)
Complete Works

Commit your way to the Lord; Trust in Him and He will do this.

Psalm 37:5 NIV

The Lord knows the proper time. Even waiting is an imperceptible advancing.

Gerhard Tersteegen (1697-1769)
Life and Writings Letter VI

The highest condition of the human will is, when, not seeing God, not seeming to grasp Him at all, we yet hold Him fast.

George Macdonald

Hiding of His face is wise love. Nay, his children must often have the frosty cold side of the hill, and set down both their bare feet among thorns. His love hath eyes, and, in the meantime, is looking on. Our pride must have winter weather to rot it!

Samuel Rutherford (1600-1661)
Letter CVII

The manifestations of God have a winter.

Samuel Rutherford (1600-1661)

Everything depends upon God's free mercy, the impartation of His influences, and the operation of His grace. Receive it therefore, consent to all that God works in you, and the attractive influence He gives you to experience, and follow this impulse, but only as far as its strength extends: then suffer, be submissive, and wait. God gives us both to will and to do according to His good pleasure; but He often imparts the will, yes, and a sincere, cordial, and fervent will too, long before He gives the power to do, or attain the wished-for object. This is painful, but at the same time a purifying humbling pain. We must eventually experience, that it is not of him that willeth; the mercy of God must grant the blessing: 'tis not our will that must seize it: for the will to do, appears sometimes to fall off, like the blossom from the tree, and to sink into a holy resignation, that room may be made for the fruit itself.

Gerhard Tersteegen (1697-1769)
Letter XV

Chapter 16

Silence

Be still and know that I am God.

Psalm 46:10
New International Version

The Lord your God is with you,
He is mighty to save.
He will take great delight in you,
He will quiet you with His love.
He will rejoice over you with singing.

Zephaniah 3:17 NIV

No eloquence in the world is half as full of meaning as the patient silence of a child of God. It is an eminent work of grace to bring down the *will* and subdue the affections to such a degree, that the whole mind lies before the Lord like the sea beneath the wind – ready to be moved by every breath of His mouth, but free from all inward and *self*-caused emotion – as also from all power to be moved by anything other than the *divine will.*

C.H. Spurgeon (1834-1892)
Treasury of David
Psalm 62:5

Shape nothing, lips; be lovely-dumb:
    It is the shut, the curfew sent
From there where all surrenders come
    Which only makes you eloquent

Gerard Manley Hopkins (1844-1889)
The Habit of Perfection

The soul that is called to a state of inward silence should not encumber itself with vocal prayers; whenever it makes use of them and finds a difficulty therein and an attraction to silence....

Madame Guyon (1648-1717)
Experiencing the Depths of Jesus Christ

There is a secret discipline appointed for every man and woman whose life is lived for others. No one escapes that discipline, nor would wish to escape it; nor can any shelter another from it. And just as we have seen the bud of a flower close round the treasure within, folding its secret up, petal by petal, so we have seen the soul that is chosen to serve, fold round its secret and hold it fast and cover it from the eyes of man. The petals of the soul are silence.

Amy Carmichael (1867-1951)
A Chance to Die

There is a silence which can only be met by silence. Silence is not a gap to be filled. It is the greatest of all preparations, and the climax of all adoration.

From the Fellowship of Silence
By various authors

Though I wished earnestly to hide nothing from Him, yet God held me so closely to Him, that I could scarcely tell anything at all.

Madame Guyon (1648-1717)
The Autobiography

Light sorrow will speak, extreme grief is dumb and cannot command one word. The deepest floods in their motion speak least, and slide down their banks without noise; shallow brooks flow with great tumbling and din. Some desires are above words, and come out in nothing but in sad sighs and deep groans.

Samuel Rutherford (1600-1661)
The Power of Faith and Prayer

I do not think there is anything from the beginning of our Christian life to the end, that is so keenly attacked as our quiet with God, for it is in quietness that we are fed. Sometimes it is not possible to get long uninterrupted quiet, but even if it be only ten minutes, "hem it with quietness": Enclose it in quietness; do not spend the time in thinking how little time you have. Be quiet. If you are interrupted, as soon as the interruption ceases, sink back into quietness again without fuss or worry of spirit. Those who know this secret and practice it are lifted up.

Amy Carmichael (1867-1951)

First, as soon as the soul by faith places itself in the presence of God, and becomes recollected before Him, let it remain thus for a little time in respectful silence.

But if, at the beginning, in forming the act of faith, it feels some little pleasing sense of the Divine presence, let it remain there without being troubled for a subject; and proceed no farther but carefully cherish this sensation while it continues. When it abates, it may excite the will by some tender affection, and if, by the first moving thereof, it finds itself reinstated in sweet peace, let it there remain. The fire must be gently fanned, but as soon as it is kindled, we must cease our efforts, lest we extinguish it by our activity.

Madame Guyon (1648-1717)
Experiencing the Depths of Jesus Christ

...With me, wheresoe'er I wander,
    That great Presence goes,
That unutterable gladness.
    Undisturbed repose.
Everywhere the blessed stillness
    Of His Holy Place –
Stillness of the love that worships
    Dumb before His face.

Gerhard Tersteegen (1697-1769)
Hymns of Tersteegen and Others from 'The Home'

He leadeth me beside the still waters.

Psalm 23:2 KJV

What are these "still waters" but the influences and graces of His blessed Spirit? His Spirit attends us in various operations, like waters – in the plural – to cleanse, to refresh, to fertilise, to cherish. They are "still waters," for the Holy Ghost loves peace, and sounds no trumpet of ostentation in His operations. He may flow into our soul, but not into our neighbors, and therefore our neighbor may not perceive the divine Presence; and though the blessed Spirit may be pouring His floods into one heart, yet he that sitteth next to the favored one may know nothing of it...that Silence is golden indeed in which the Holy Spirit meets with the souls of saints.

C.H. Spurgeon (1834-1892)
Songs of David
23 Psalm v.2

Within The Holiest

His priest am I, before Him day and night,
    Within His Holy Place;
And death, and life, and all things dark and bright,
    I spread before His Face.
Rejoicing with His joy, yet ever still,
    For silence is my song;
My work to bend beneath His blessed will,
    All day, and all night long –
Forever holding with Him converse sweet,
    Yet <u>speechless</u>, for my gladness is complete.

Gerhard Tersteegen (1697-1769)
Hymns of Tersteegen and Others

...There, Lord, to lose, in bliss of Thine embrace
    The recreant will;
There, in the radiance of Thy blessed face,
    Be hushed and still;
There, speechless at Thy pierced feet
    See none and nought beside,
And know but this – that Thou art sweet,
    That I am satisfied.

Gerhard Tersteegen
From "At Last"

Chapter 17

Prayer

*Lord 'teach us to pray' is itself
a good prayer.*

Matthew Henry's Commentary
Luke 11:1

Since the first day that you set your mind to gain understanding and to humble yourself before your Lord – your words were heard.

Daniel 10:12 NIV

What God will give, He inclines the hearts of His praying people to ask, and for what He will do, He will be enquired of.

Matthew Henry (1662-1715)

The earnest (heartfelt, continued) prayer of a righteous man makes tremendous power available (dynamic in its working).

James 5:16 Amplified

And when they wanted wine, the Mother of Jesus saith unto Him, "They have no wine."

John 2:3 KJV

She acquaints Him with the difficulty they were in: She saith unto Him, they have no wine. In our addresses to Christ, we must not prescribe to Him, but humbly spread out our case before Him, and then refer ourselves to do as He pleases.

Matthew Henry (1662-1715)
Matthew Henry's Commentary John 2:3

I pour out my complaint before Him; I tell Him my trouble.

Psalm 142:2 NIV

Even good men may ask for temporal blessings, and not receive them; because the things we suppose good, may not <u>be</u> good, or not good for <u>us</u>, or not good for us <u>at present</u>. But none shall seek God for the <u>best</u> of blessings in vain. If we ask enough, we shall have it.

Thomas Case (1598-1682)
The Treasury of David

Open thy mouth wide, and I will fill it.

Psalm 81:10 KJV

There may be no crying with the voice where there is vehement praying, as Hanah prayed and poured out her soul before the Lord (1 Samuel 1:15). This was heart crying. *Now Hanah, she spake in her heart; only her lips moved, but her voice was not heard.* (verse 13)

There may be much praying where there is no crying. In some prayers, there is much tongue, little spirit and life; so, in some others there is much spirit, little tongue. Light sorrow will speak, extreme grief is dumb and cannot command one word.

Samuel Rutherford (1600-1661)
The Power of Faith and Prayer

I see now that we cannot enter into the fullness of the confidence of 1 John 5:14-15 and say without any shade of mental reservation, "We know that we have," unless our prayer is for God's greatest gift – spiritual triumph. This triumph is not deliverance <u>from</u>, but victory <u>in</u> trial, and that not intermittent but perpetual.

Settle this in your minds so that you will not have to settle it again; there is no promise of ease for any soldier on any field. Search the New Testament; you will not find one such promise. It is made quite clear that things are not going to be made easy. So to be surprised and troubled when they are difficult is foolish and unreasonable too. Why is there so much inward stress, sometimes sharp trial, or what the New Testament calls Tribulation? We are not told; but we are told that there *will* be this sort of thing, and that it is "not worthy to be compared with the glory."

Amy Carmichael (1867-1951)
Edges of His Ways

A sovereign elixir * full of virtue may be given in a few drops; so a little prayer – if it be with the heart and the spirit, may have much virtue and efficacy * in it.

Thomas Watson (1620-1686)
A Body of Divinity

* a powerful invigorating remedy   * power – effectiveness

God, have mercy on me, a sinner.

Luke 18:13 NIV

Have mercy upon me, O Lord; for I am weak; O Lord, heal me; for my bones are vexed.

Psalm 6:2 KJV

...But coming before God the most forcible argument that ye can use is your necessity, poverty, tears, misery, unworthiness, and confessing them to Him, it shall be an open door to furnish you with all things that He hath...The tears of our misery are forcible arrows to pierce the heart of our heavenly Father, to deliver us and to pity our hard case.

Archibald Symson
The Treasury of David

Prayer is as various as life. There is a prayer that is swift, brief, a look, a thought; there is the long drawn out prayer of long tension; the prayer whose instant first answer is peace; the prayer that is just the pouring out of the heart – "Lord, all my desire is before Thee" – And as to that desire, love does not need to explain itself to Love.

But though this be so, I have been thinking today of the kind of prayer that sooner or later we must learn to pray for one another. We must learn to pray more for *spiritual victory* than from protection against battle wounds, relief from their havoc, rest from their pain. We must reach the place where we bend all our prayers that way or (for I do want to be honest) our chief prayers. Love cannot be without longing to shield and to relieve, for Love is of God, so we may be at rest about this inseparable instinct and quality of love, for Love understands.

Amy Carmichael (1867-1951)
Edges of His Ways

As for God, His way is perfect.

Psalm 18:30 KJV

I have been thinking much of this word. We say it, we write it but the love of God is searching; and it seems to me that all our lives long He is patiently teaching us to truly mean it.

We make plans after much prayer and long waiting. They are on the edge of fulfilment and then something happens to shatter them. If they affected our lives only, it would be easy to say "His way is perfect," but if others must suffer, then it is not easy to say those words in sincerity. God knows this. He does not hurry us, but He does wait for us. He waits in patience till we can look in His face and say – not with a sigh, but with a song – "As for God, His way is perfect." This is victory, nothing less can be called by that shining name.

Amy Carmichael (1867-1951)
Edges of His Ways

I believe that if we are to be and do for others what God means us to be and to do, we must not let <u>Adoration and worship</u> slip into second place, for it is the central service asked by God of human souls; and its neglect is responsible for much lack of spiritual depth and power. Perhaps we may find here the reason why we so often run dry. We do not give time enough to what makes for depth, and so we are shallow; a wind, quite a little wind, can ruffle our surface, a little hot sun and all the moisture in us evaporates. It should not be so.

.....Today, if we will hear His voice, today, this morning, if we will draw near to Him, He will draw near to us. In the hush of that nearness, we shall not seek anything for ourselves, not even help, or light, or comfort; we shall forget ourselves, "lost in wonder, love, and praise."

Amy Carmichael (1867-1951)
Edges of His Ways

Every day [with its new reasons] will I bless you [affectionately and gratefully praise You]; yes, I will praise Your name forever and ever.

Psalm 145:2 Expanded

This morning I feasted on a very familiar word, but it came freshly. (John 17:20 NIV) *'Neither for these only do I pray, but for them also that believe on Me through their word.'*

How much we value the prayers of one another, how dear they are to us. But His are dearer, far more precious. Oh, what manner of people we should be, prayed for by our Lord Himself!

Amy Carmichael (1867-1951)
Candles in the Dark

It is God who justifies – Who is he that condemns? Christ Jesus, who died – more than that, who was raised to life – is at the right hand of God and is also interceding for us.

Romans 8:33, 34 NIV

That God has promised to give us what we ask of Him...*Ask and it shall be given you,* either the thing itself you shall ask or that which is equivalent; either the thorn in the flesh removed or grace sufficient given.

Matthew Henry (1662-1715)
Commentary

Think through me, thoughts of God,
My Father, quiet me,
Till in Thy holy presence, hushed.
I think Thy thoughts with Thee.

Think through me, Thoughts of God,
That always, everywhere,
The stream that through my being, flows,
May homeward pass in prayer.

Think through me, Thoughts of God,
And let my own thoughts be
Lost like the sand-pools on the shore
Of the eternal sea.

Amy Carmichael (1867-1951)
Toward Jerusalem

And this is the confidence that we have in Him, that if we ask anything according to His will, He heareth us: And if we know that He heareth us, whatsoever we ask, we know that we have the petitions that we desired of Him.

1 John 5:14-15 KJV

Love gave us these words and only love can understand them. One who loves his Father knows by a kind of Heavenly instinct what he may ask for, and what he may not ask for. Or if he be in any doubt, he ceases to ask anything and rests his heart on His Lord's own prayer, "Thy will be done." So it is that he has this confidence, and knows that he has the petitions that he has desired of Him.

The words are not for casual use, or for any except those who earnestly want to be His true lovers, to whom the lightest wish of their Lord is a command. The least of us may be a lover.

Amy Carmichael (1867-1951)
Edges of His Ways

That is the surest faith and most abiding that has pure
God in Christ and naked omnipotence and infinite
mercy for its formal object – not God as clothed with
means, creatures and second causes that He works by.

Samuel Rutherford (1600-1661)
The Power of Faith and Prayer

Away despair! My gracious Lord doth hear;
Though winds and waves assault my keel.
He doth preserve it. He doth steer.
Even when the boat seems most to reel
Storms are the triumph of His art;
Well may He close His eyes, but not His heart.....

George Herbert (1593-1633)
from The Bag
The Poems of George Herbert

Chapter 18

Prayers that God Hears

This is the confidence that we have in approaching God: that if we ask anything according to His will, He hears us. And if we know that He hears us – whatever we ask – we know that we have what we asked for.

1 John 14-15 NIV

Paul's Prayers For Me

Dear Lord, fill me with the knowledge of Your will through all spiritual wisdom and understanding. Help me to live a life worthy of You, Lord. Help me to please You in every way, to bear fruit in every good work, to grow in knowledge of You, to be strengthened with all power according to Your glorious might so that I may have great endurance and patience.

Colossians 1:9-11 NIV

Paul's Prayers For Me

Dear Lord, strengthen my heart so that I will be blameless and holy in your presence, my God and my Father, when our Lord Jesus comes with all His holy ones.

from II Thessalonians 3:13 NIV

In your hands are strength and power to exalt and give strength to all.

I Chronicles 29:12 NIV

Paul's Prayers For Me

Lord, you are the God of Hope. Fill me, with all joy and peace as I trust in You, so that I may overflow with hope by the power of the Holy Spirit.

Romans 15:13 NIV

But the Lord's unfailing love surrounds the man who trusts in Him.

Psalm 32:10 NIV

Paul's Prayers for Anyone

May _____
      be able to discern what is best
      be pure and blameless
      be filled with the fruit of righteousness
      live a life worthy of You
      please You in every way
      bear fruit in every good work
      overflow with hope as _____trust(s)
      in You
      whole body be kept blameless

Help _____to obey You

May the Lord be _____ confidence and
keep _____ foot from being snared.

Paul's Prayers for Anyone

I pray that out of your glorious riches You may strengthen _____ with power, through Your Spirit in _____'s heart through faith. And I pray that _____ being rooted and established in love, may have power, together with all the saints, to grasp how wide and long and high and deep is the love of Christ, and to know this love that surpasses knowledge – that _____ may be filled to the measure of all the fullness of God.

Ephesians 3:14-19

Paul's Prayers for Anyone

Fill _____ with a knowledge of Your will through all spiritual wisdom and understanding

May _____ grow in knowledge of You

May You be glorified in _____ and _____ in You

Strengthen _____ with power through Your Spirit in _____ inner being so that Christ may dwell in _____ heart through faith

Help _____ to obey You

Deliver _____ from evil

Lead _____ not into temptation

Guide _____ in the path of righteousness

Paul's Prayers for Anyone

And this is my prayer: that _____ love may abound more and more in knowledge and depth of insight, so that _____ may be able to discern what is best and may be pure and blameless until the day of Christ, filled with the fruit of righteousness that comes through Jesus Christ – to the glory and praise of God.

Philippians 1:9-11 NIV

Paul's Prayers for Anyone

Glorious Father, please give _____ the Spirit of wisdom and revelation so that _____ may know You better. I pray also that the eyes of _____'s heart may be enlightened in order that _____ may know the hope to which You have called _____, the riches of your glorious inheritance in the saints and your incomparably great power for us who believe.

Ephesians 1:7

To God belong wisdom and power; counsel and understanding are His.

Job 12:13 NIV

Paul's Prayers for Anyone

Sanctify _____ through and through

Strengthen _____ in every good deed and word

Equip _____ with everything good for doing Your will

Work in _____ what is pleasing to You

Count _____ worthy of Your calling

Fulfill every good purpose of _____ and every act prompted by _____'s faith

John 17: What Jesus Prays for His disciples, we can pray for our church

May God be glorified in our church
Protect us by the power of your name
May You reveal yourself to us that we may all know you
Strengthen our belief
May those You send to us believe
May none of our flock be lost
May we be one
May we be brought to complete unity
Help us to obey you
Sanctify us by the truth

Please make righteousness and praise spring up in our little church before all nations.

Chapter 19

Facing Tragedy and Death

*The Lord is close to the brokenhearted
and saves those who are crushed in spirit.*

Psalm 34:18
New International Version

Such as are in prosperity, and are fatted with earthly joys, and increased with children and friends, though the Word of God is indeed written to such for their instruction, yet to you, who are in trouble (spare me, Madam, to say this), from whom the Lord hath taken many children, and whom He hath exercised otherwise;, there are some chapters, some particular promises in the Word of God, made in a most special manner, which should never have been yours, so as they are, if you had your portion in this life, as others. And therefore, all the comforts, promises, and mercies God offereth to the afflicted, they are as so many love letters written to you. Take them to you, Madam, and claim your right, and be not robbed. It is no small comfort, that God hath written some scriptures to you, which He hath not written to others. Ye seem rather in this to be envied than pittied; and ye are indeed in this like people of another world, and those that are above the ordinary rank of mankind, whom, our King and Lord, our Bridegroom Jesus in His love letter to His well-beloved spouse, hath named beside all the rest.....and think your God is like a friend that sendeth a letter to a whole house and family, but speaketh in His letter to some by name, that are dearest to Him in the house.

Samuel Rutherford (1600-1661)
Letter XLII

The Spirit of the Sovereign Lord is on me, because the Lord has anointed me to preach good news to the poor...to comfort all who mourn, and provide for those who grieve in Zion – to bestow on them a crown of beauty instead of ashes, the oil of gladness instead of mourning, and a garment of praise instead of a spirit of despair...

Isaiah 61:1-3 NIV

...It is then best for us, in the obedience of faith, and in holy submission, to give that to God which the law of His almighty and just power will have of us. Therefore Madame, your Lord wills you, in all states of life, to say, "Thy will be done in earth as it is in heaven:" and herein shall ye have comfort, - that He, who sees perfectly through all your evils, and knows the frame and constitution of your nature, and what is most healthful for your soul, - holds every cup of affliction to your head, with His own gracious hand. Never believe that your tender-hearted Savior, who knows the strength of your stomach, will mix that cup with one drop of poison. Drink then, with the patience of the saints, and the God of patience bless your physic. (medicine)

Samuel Rutherford (1600-1661)
Letter III to Lady Kenmure 1628

-upon the death of his darling little daughter, Ann- "I desire to see in it a Father's authority who may do what He will, and a Father's love who may do what is best."

Matthew Henry's Father
Biography in Commentary on the Whole Bible

He is the Lord; let Him do what is good in His eyes.

1 Sam 3:18 NIV

Let this comfort those whom Christ loves – under all their grievances, that the design of them all is that the Son of God may be glorified. Thereby, His wisdom, power, and goodness, is glorified in supporting and relieving them.

Matthew Henry (1662 – 1715)
Commentary

No fear of our suffering from too much of an overflowing cup if He fills it, and we take it from His hand, looking all the while in His face. He knows best what to give. 'Your heavenly Father knoweth' has a store of comfort in it.

Andrew Bonar (1810-1892)
Heavenly Springs

I know your Ladyship thinketh yourself little in the common of this world, for the favorable aspect of any of these three painted faces (honour, riches, pleasures), and blessed be our Lord that is so. The better for you, Madam; they are not worthy to be wooers, to suit in marriage your soul, that look to no higher match than to be married upon painted clay. Know, therefore, Madam, the place wither our Lord Jesus cometh to woo a bride, it is even in the furnace: for if ye be one of Zion's daughters ... the Lord, who hath His fire in Zion, and His furnace in Jerusalem (Isa. 31:9) is purifying you in the furnace. And therefore be content to live in it, and everyday to be adding and sewing – to a pasement* to your wedding garment, that ye may be at last decored and trimmed as a bride for Christ, a bride of His own busking*, beautified in the hidden man of the heart.

Samuel Rutherford (1600-1661))
Letter XLII 1634

* strip of lace
* busk – adorn, deck

Build your nest on no tree here; for ye see God hath sold the forest to death and every tree where upon we would rest is ready to be cut down.

Samuel Rutherford (1600-1661)
Letters

Incense Trees

...Photographs show a blistered land, naked in the sun, covered for miles with sand, broken stones, or bare rock, almost waterless, almost treeless. But one of the high roads of the Old World, the trade route from India and Persia to Egypt and Syria, and to other countries round the Mediterranean, ran through this Hazamaveth, and it supplied its own fragrant contribution to that ancient-world commerce, a contribution not great in extent but vast in significance.

Incense trees grew along the barren plateau and in the dry riverbeds. Merchants came from as far away as Persia to find this precious gum. The Frankincense and myrrh the wise men offered to our Savior may have grown in that burning land, and that which gave fragrance to the ointment Mary poured upon His hair and His feet, and the spices that the women laid among the linen for His burying. But the chief thought with me today is that this substance, universal symbol of prayer, worship, and adoration, was found in such a place. There is a touch of wonder in that, as in all the thoughts of God. Sooner or later we find ourselves in some Hazarmaveth of His appointment. We may miss the incense trees or we may find them. If we miss them we shall not find them anywhere else.

Amy Carmichael (1867-1951)
Rose from Briar

And as to what are your fears about the health or life of your dear children, lay it upon Christ's shoulders: let Him bear all. Loose your grips of them all; and when your dear Lord pulleth, let them go with faith and joy. It is a tried faith to kiss a Lord that is taking from you.

Samuel Rutherford (1600-1661)
Letters March 19, 1632

Jesu! Close our eyes in life and death that we may no longer contemplate ourselves and what regards us, but commit ourselves nakedly, blindly, and entirely unto Thee, assenting willingly and sincerely to our own nothingness and thus – in the artless carelessness of faith, live and die with Thee and in Thee.

Gerhard Tersteegen (1697-1769)
August 29, 1741

No affliction would trouble a child of God, if he knew God's reason for sending it.

At Dawn of Day
Jan 13

In times of great suffering, grieving people often pose a challenge to any minister within earshot: "Why did God allow this evil to happen?" To answer that question, a pastor must develop a theodicy (i.e., a response that justifies belief in an all-loving and all-powerful God in spite of sin and evil). Although the existence and extent of evil is a profound mystery, the message of Christianity shines through even in darkness. According to the Bible, **not even God** exempted Himself from the agony of human suffering. The second Person of the Trinity, Jesus Christ, God of very God, experienced a gruesome encounter with pain and agony on the cross.

This very truth struck Rev. Edward Shillito, as he watched wave after wave of wounded young men return from the First World War. How could Christianity still be "good news" to those who had seen the slaughter of brutal trench warfare in the European theatre of battle? Shillito, a Free Church minister in England, saw a partial reply in the following teaching: among all the world religions, only Christianity portrays a God suffering as a man. The following poem, *Jesus of the Scars*, was his attempt to explain this clearly comforting truth in a world wracked by war, death, injustice, and natural disasters.

Jesus of the Scars

If we have never sought we seek Thee now.
Thine eyes burn through the dark, our only stars;
We must have sight of thorn pricks on Thy brow,
We must have Thee, O Jesus of the Scars.

The heavens frighten us; they are too calm.
In all the universe we have no place.
Our wounds are hurting us – where is the balm?
Lord Jesus, by Thy scars, we claim Thy grace.

The other gods were strong, but thou wast weak.
They rode, but Thou dids't stumble to a throne.
But to our wounds, only God's wounds, can speak.
And not a god has wounds, but Thou alone!

Edward Shillito (1872-1948)

Ye have now Madam, a sickness before you, and also after that a death. Gather now food for the journey. God give you eyes to see something beyond death. I doubt not, but that, if hell were betwixt you and Christ, as a river which ye behoved to cross ere you should come at Him, but ye would willingly put in your foot, and make through to be at Him, upon hope that He would come in Himself, in the deepest of the river, and lend you His hand. Now I believe your hell is dried up, and you have only these two shallow brooks, sickness and death, to pass through; and yet have also a promise that Christ shall do more than meet you, even that He shall come Himself, and go with you foot for foot, yea and bear you in His arms. O then! O then! For the joy that is set before you; for the love of the Man (who is also "God over all, blessed forever"), that is standing upon the shore to welcome you, run your race with patience. The Lord go with you.

Samuel Rutherford (1600-1661)
Letter III to the Viscountess of Kenmure

When you pass through the waters, I will be with you, and when you pass through the rivers, they will not sweep over you.

Isaiah 43:2 NIV

....Gladness and joy will overtake them and sorrow and sighing will flee away.

Isaiah 35:10 NIV

Though

Let spirit conquer, though the flesh
Be strong to prison and enmesh.

And though the Shining Summit be
Far, far from me, Lord, far from me,

And though black precipices frown
"O let me climb when I lye down."*

Amy Carmichael (1867-1951)

* Henry Vaughn (1622-1695)

Oil and Wine

There is a balm for every pain,
 A medicine for all sorrow;
The eye turned backward to the Cross;
 And forward to the morrow.
The morrow of the glory and the psalm,
 When He shall come;
The morrow of the harping and the palm,
 The welcome home.
Meantime in His beloved hands our ways,
And on His Heart the wandering heart at rest;
And comfort for the weary one who lays
 His head upon His breast.

Gerhard Tersteegen (1697-1769)
The Hymns of Tersteegen and others

As a Mother comforts her child, so will I comfort you.

Isaiah 66:13 NIV

Wilt Love Me? Trust Me? Praise Me?

O thou beloved child of My desire,
Whether I lead thee through green valleys,
  By still waters, or through fire,
Or lay thee down in silence under snow,
Through any weather, and whatever
  Cloud may gather, wind may blow –
Wilt love Me? trust Me? Praise Me?

No gallant bird, O dearest Lord, am I,
That anywhere, in any weather,
  Rising singeth; Low I lie.
And yet I cannot fear, for I shall soar,
Thy love shall wing me, blessed Savior;
  So I shall answer, I adore,
I love Thee, trust Thee, praise Thee.

Amy Carmichael (1867-1951)
Toward Jerusalem

O thrice fools are we, who, like new-born princes weeping in the cradle, know not that there is a Kingdom before them.

Samuel Rutherford (1600-1661)
Letter XX

After this I looked, and there before me was a door standing open in heaven.

Revelation 4:1 NIV

I want to live looking through that door, living as one who truly believes that the temporal matters not at all; only the Eternal is important.

Amy Carmichael (1867-1951)
Thou Givest – They Gather

I want to live in the light of the thought of His coming, His triumph – the end of this present darkness, the glory of His seen Presence. This bathes the present in radiance. You won't be sorry then that you trusted when you couldn't see, when neither sun nor stars in many days appeared and no small tempest lay on you (Acts 27:20). No, you won't be sorry then. So don't be sorry now. I am believing. 'All joy and peace in believing': the words ring out like a chime of bells.

Amy Carmichael (1867-1951)
Candles in the Dark

...Not that He doth explain
The mystery that baffleth; but a sense
Hushéd the quiet heart, that far, far hence
Lieth a field set thick with golden grain,
Wetted in seedling days by many a rain;
The End, it will explain.

Amy Carmichael (1867-1951)
From The End

My dear brother – let God make of you what He will.
He will end all with consolation, and make glory out of
your sufferings, and would you wish for better work?

Samuel Rutherford (1600 – 1661)
Letters

Finis

When Herod realized that he had been outwitted by the Magi, he was furious, and he gave orders to kill all the boys in Bethlehem and its vicinity who were two years old and under....

Matthew 2:16 NIV

To the Infant Martyrs

Go smiling souls, your new built cages break,
In Heav'n you'll learn to sing ere here to speak,
Nor let the milky fonts that bathe your thirst,
    Be your delay;
The place that calls you hence, is at the worst
    Milk all the way.

Richard Crashaw (1612-1649)

Notes 276

.